DISCARD

Make a Joyful Noise!

The Big Book of
Christian Crafts

The Big Book of

Christian Crafts

Kathy Ross

Illustrated by Sharon Lane Holm

The Millbrook Press   Brookfield, Connecticut

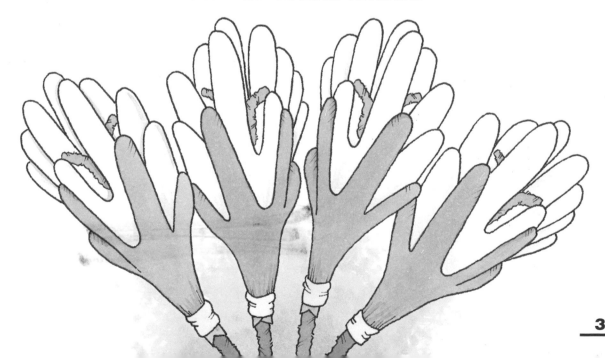

For Julianna Katharine

With special thanks to Patti M. Hummel and the Benchmark Group

Library of Congress Control Number: 2001135504

ISBN 0-7613-1594-2

Published by The Millbrook Press, Inc.
2 Old New Milford Road
Brookfield, Connecticut 06804
www.millbrookpress.com

Contents

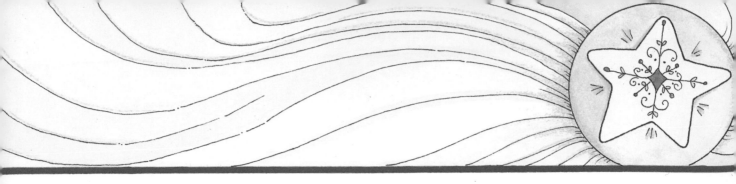

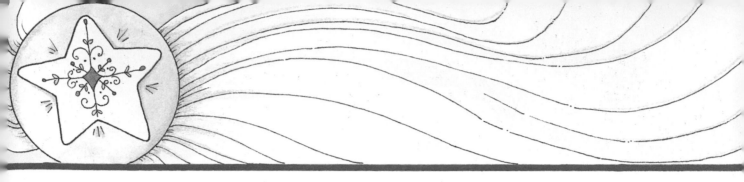

Dear Reader,

I have always been a hands-on learner. My understanding of not only stories, but also ideas, increases when I am an active participant in the learning process. I suspect the same to be true for many children. And so, I wrote this book to help parents and teachers help children to help themselves learn.

The crafts come from my many years of teaching preschool and Sunday school. They range from very specific projects that demonstrate Bible stories, to crafts that convey concepts that teach Christian values and behavior. A section of the book that is particularly important to me is the one on Christmas. All of the projects focus on the true meaning of the holiday as the birth day of Jesus, and avoid the secular symbols that have built up around the celebration. The final section contains projects that express the joy of being a Christian.

I am a teacher, not an artist, and the projects are simple enough to assure that all children will be able to have a satisfying creative experience. Also, there is little or no cost involved. Most of the projects are made from simple household materials, many of them recycled, and only an occasional small craft item (such as a wiggle eye) that can usually be substituted.

So, whether you are having a quiet rainy afternoon with one child, or teaching a large Sunday school class, the crafts will work as they have for the many children I've been blessed to share them with over the years.

Kathy Ross

In the Beginning

The story of how God created the
world and everything in it is told in the
very first chapter of the first book
of the Bible (Genesis 1:1).
CREATION WHEEL 10

God made the earth we live on.
GLUE AND TISSUE EARTH 12

God turns the night to day.
NIGHT TO DAY WHEEL 14

God covered the earth with water.
WATER COVERING THE EARTH 16

God brought the dry land up out of the water.
DRY LAND APPEARING 18

God made trees to grow on the dry land.
TREE WITH SQUIRREL PUPPET 20

God made the many different plants that grow.
GROWING PLANT 22

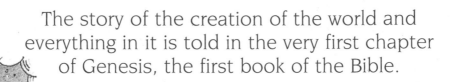

The story of the creation of the world and everything in it is told in the very first chapter of Genesis, the first book of the Bible.

Creation Wheel

you need:

scissors

pencil

ruler

corrugated cardboard

light-weight cardboard

markers

white glue

cotton ball

paper fastener

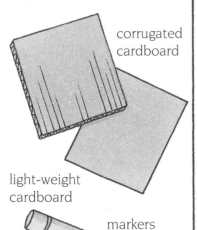

what you do:

1 Cut a 12-inch (30-cm) circle from the corrugated cardboard. Cut an identical circle from the light-weight cardboard.

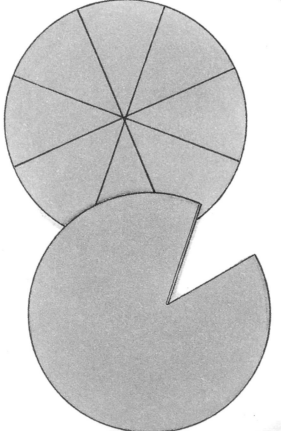

2 Use the ruler to divide the corrugated cardboard circle into eight equal wedge-shaped segments. Cut a segment from the light-weight cardboard that is slightly smaller than one segment of the corrugated cardboard circle. Make sure it does not go all the way to the center of the light-weight cardboard circle.

3 Use the markers to decorate each segment on the corrugated cardboard to tell about the seven days of creation. In the <u>first segment</u> write "The Story of Creation" and decorate the segment. The next segment will be the <u>first day</u> of creation, when God separated the light from the dark. On the <u>second day</u> He made the sky. You can glue a bit of cotton in the sky to look like clouds. On the <u>third day</u> He separated the lands from the seas, and on the <u>fourth day</u> God put the sun, the moon, and the stars in the sky. On the <u>fifth day</u> He filled the seas with fish and the sky with birds. On the <u>sixth day</u> He created all the animals and He created man. On the <u>seventh day</u> God rested from his work.

4 Attach the light-weight cardboard circle to the top of the corrugated cardboard circle by putting the paper fastener through the center of both circles. Arrange the top circle so that the title segment, "The Story of Creation," shows through.

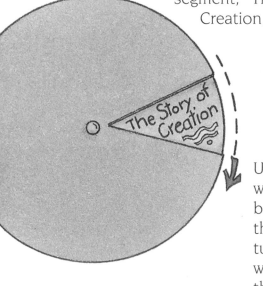

Use the creation wheel to tell the biblical story of the creation, turning the top wheel to expose the picture of each of the seven days.

Glue and Tissue Earth

you need:

white tissue paper

blue and green
colored craft glue

pin

wire or string

scissors

Styrofoam tray to work on

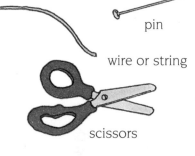

what you do:

1 Cut two 1-foot-square (30-cm) pieces of tissue paper. Place them on the Styrofoam tray.

2 Squeeze a 5-inch (13-cm) circle of blue glue onto the paper. Fill in the circle with blue glue. This will be the water on the earth.

3 Squeeze some green glue over the blue glue down the center of the earth for landforms.

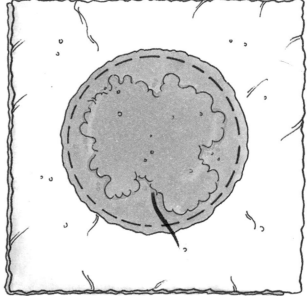

4 Carefully set the second square of tissue over the glue earth on the first square of tissue. Let the glue dry completely. This can take several days. After a couple of days, if you have sealed pockets of glue, poke the pockets in two or three places with a pin so that the air can get in to dry the glue.

5 When the glue has dried completely, cut out the earth in a circle, using a small plate or bowl as a pattern. Trim away any rough edges of glue.

6 Poke a hole in the top of the earth with the pin or the end of the wire. Thread wire or string through the hole and twist or tie the ends together to make a hanger for the earth.

This project looks especially pretty hanging in a window with the sun shining through it.

Thank you, God, for our earth.

God turns the night to day.

Night to Day Wheel

you need:

two 9-inch (23-cm) uncoated paper plates

black and blue poster paints plus two other colors

paintbrush

yellow construction paper

sticker stars

white glue

scissors

fiberfill

yarn, doilies, and other collage materials

paper fastener

what you do:

1 Cut a window about 3 inches (8 cm) tall and 4 inches (10 cm) wide in the top half of one of the paper plates.

2 Paint half of the eating side of the other paper plate black for the night sky. Paint the remaining half blue for the day sky.

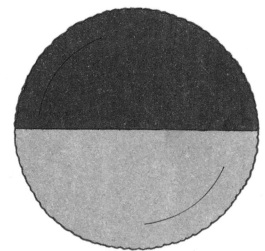

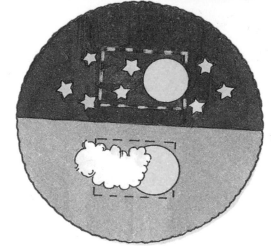

3 Cut a 1 1/2-inch (3.75-cm) circle from the yellow construction paper. This will be the moon. Glue it in the night sky, making sure it will be visible through the window cut in the top plate. Glue sticker stars around the moon. Use glue, even though the stars are self-stick, so that they will not rub off when turning the sky from night to day.

4 Cut a 2-inch (5-cm) circle from the yellow paper for the sun. Glue the sun on the blue-sky portion of the plate, making sure it will be visible through the window cut in the top plate. Glue some wisps of fiberfill over one side of the sun for the clouds.

5 Paint around the window with poster paint for the walls. Paint a floor below the window using a different color paint.

6 Use the yarn, doilies, and other collage materials to decorate the "room."

7 Place the window plate over the sky plate and fasten them together with a paper fastener through the center of the two plates.

To change the night to day, just turn the back plate around to show the day sky.

Thank you, God, for the night to rest and the day to learn more about your love.

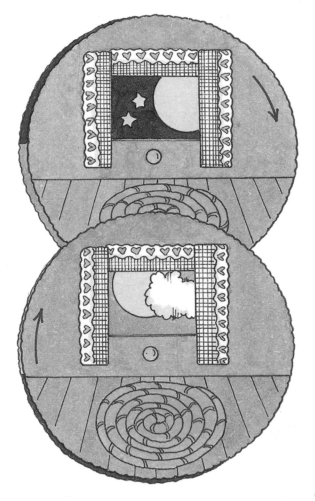

God covered the earth with water.

Water Covering the Earth

you need:

12- by 18-inch (30- by 46-cm) construction paper, 2 black and 1 brown

stapler

sticker stars

white glue

glitter

blue plastic wrap

paper reinforcers

hole punch

yarn

scissors

what you do:

1 Cut a 5-inch (13-cm) circle out of the center of one of the sheets of black paper. This will be for the earth. Staple the two sheets of black paper together along the top and bottom edges, with the sheet with the hole cut in it on top.

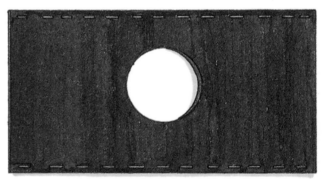

2 Glue sticker stars and glitter on the paper around the hole to look like outer space.

3 Staple a 6-inch (15-cm)-wide strip of blue plastic wrap to the left side of the brown paper. This will be the water. Fold the top and bottom edges of the brown paper up 1 inch (2.5 cm) and use staples to secure the folds. Punch a hole in the center of the left edge of the brown paper. Secure the hole with a paper reinforcer. Cut a 2-foot (60-cm) length of yarn. String one end of the yarn through the hole and tie the two ends together.

4 Leaving 6 inches (15 cm) of brown paper to the left of the plastic wrap, trim off the rest of the right side of the brown paper. Punch a hole in the center of the right side of the paper. Secure it with a hole reinforcer. Cut a second 2-foot length of yarn. String the end through the hole and tie the two ends together.

5 Slide the brown paper in between the two pieces of the black paper so that the blue plastic wrap is hidden on the left and the brown paper shows through the hole. The yarn ties should stick out on each side to pull. Staple the sides of the black paper together above and below the ties.

Show the earth being covered with water by pulling on the right tie to bring the blue plastic wrap into sight.

Thank you, God, for giving us water.

God brought the dry land up
out of the water.

Dry Land Appearing

you need:

12- by 18-inch (30- by 60-cm) sheet of light-blue construction paper

stapler

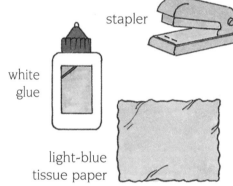

white glue

light-blue tissue paper

brown construction paper

straw

scissors

what you do:

1 Fold up about 6 inches (15 cm) of the short side of the blue construction paper. Staple the sides of the fold to make a pocket. Cover the outside of the fold with glue. Then crumple a piece of blue tissue paper into the glue to make the water. Just keep pushing the tissue into the glue until it fits over the folded area exactly.

2 Cut a small triangle-shaped piece out of the bottom of the fold.

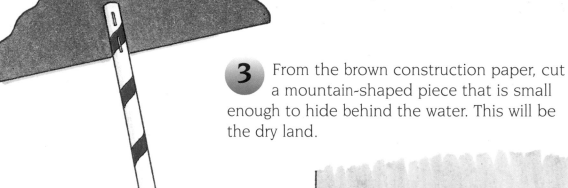

3 From the brown construction paper, cut a mountain-shaped piece that is small enough to hide behind the water. This will be the dry land.

4 Staple the dry land to the end of the straw. Slip the other end of the straw into the pocket and cut out the piece from the bottom of the pocket so that the land is hidden behind the water.

Make the dry land appear by pushing on the bottom of the straw.

Thank you, God, for the dry land.

God made trees to grow
on the dry land.

Tree With
Squirrel Puppet

you need:

scissors

cardboard
toilet-tissue
tube

brown and green
tissue paper

white glue

black permanent
marker

brown marker top

what you do:

1 Cut a 1-inch (2.5-cm) hole out of the side of the bottom part of the tube. This will be the hole for the squirrel.

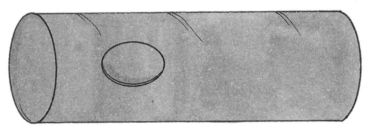

2 Cover the tube with glue, then wrap it in brown tissue paper. The tissue should not be put on smoothly, but with lots of bumps and wrinkles to look like real tree bark.

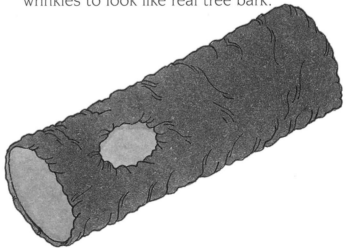

3 Cut three 6-inch (15-cm) square pieces of green tissue paper. Stack them with the corners all going in different directions. Cover the inside of the top of the tree tube with glue. Push the center portion of the green squares down into the treetop so that the green sticks out around the tree for leaves.

4 Use the black marker to draw a squirrel face, paws, and tail on the brown marker top, with the head at the top of the cap.

Put the squirrel on your finger and stick it up through the bottom of the tree to peek out the hole.

Thank you, God, for the trees.

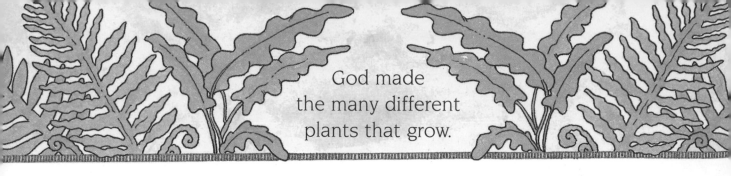

God made
the many different
plants that grow.

Growing Plant

you need:

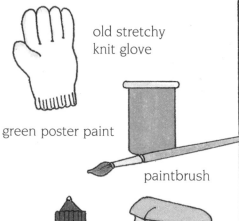

old stretchy
knit glove

green poster paint

paintbrush

white
glue

stapler

brown
construction
paper

trims

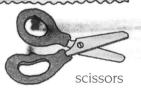

scissors

Styrofoam tray
to work on

what you do:

1 If the glove is not already green, paint its entire outside green and let it dry on the Styrofoam tray. You do not need to paint the cuff of the glove because it will not show.

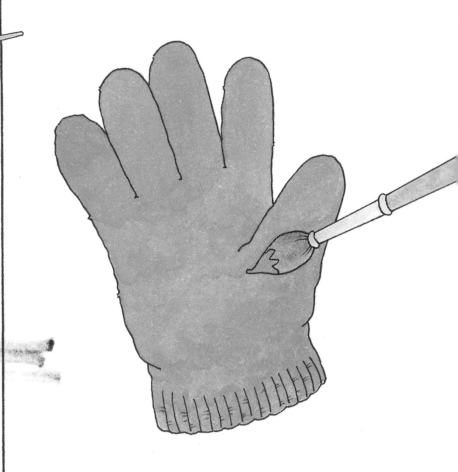

2 Fold the construction paper in half. Starting at the fold, cut a flowerpot shape that is at least 6 inches (15 cm) wide at the bottom and 6 inches tall. Cut along the bottom fold of the pot so you have a front and back piece. Staple the two pieces together along the two sides of the pot.

3 Decorate the paper pot by gluing on rows of pretty trim.

To use the plant puppet, put the green glove on your hand and then slip your hand up in the bottom of the pot. Make the plant "grow" by slowly pushing the glove up through the top of the pot.

Thank you, God, for the plants that grow.

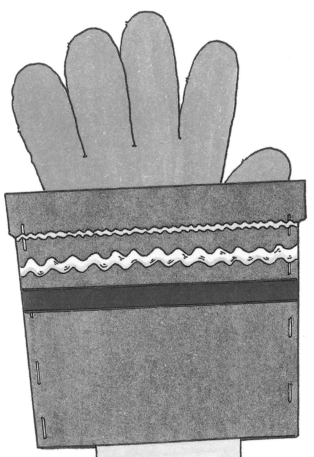

God filled the air with birds.

Flying Bird

you need:

light paper

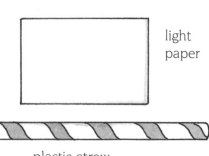
plastic straw

cellophane tape

scissors

white glue

markers

feather fluffs

what you do:

1 Cut a 4- by 2-inch (10- by 5-cm) piece of paper. Roll the paper loosely around one end of the straw and secure with tape. It must be able to slip easily off the straw.

Slip the roll off the straw and fold the end into a

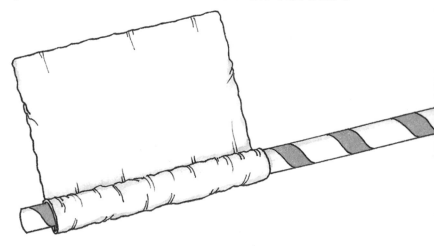

2 point. Secure the point with tape if you need to. The lighter the bird the farther it will fly, so use as little tape as possible.

3 Use markers to color a beak on the point and draw on eyes.

4 Glue on two small feather fluffs for wings. Add some snips of feather to the back of the bird for the tail.

To fly the bird, slide the bird over the end of the straw. Aim the bird skyward and blow hard in the other end of the straw.

Thank you, God, for the birds.

God filled the waters with fish and other creatures.

Bottom of the Sea Diorama

you need:

disposable plastic container with green or blue top

pipe cleaners

masking tape

gold glitter

scissors

tiny wiggle eyes

white glue

buttons

cellophane tape

shredded cellophane or paper grass

tiny black beads

thread

what you do:

1 Cut a 3-inch (8-cm) piece of green pipe cleaner. Wrap smaller pieces of pipe cleaner around the pipe cleaner piece to make a seaweed plant. Bend an inch of the bottom of the plant to the side and use masking tape to secure it to the bottom of the container.

2 Cover the bottom of the inside of the container with glue. Sprinkle the glue with gold glitter to look like the sandy ocean bottom.

3 Glue some grass to one side of the container for a different kind of seaweed.

4 Make a tiny crab by stringing the two ends of a 2-inch (5-cm) pipe cleaner piece down through two holes of a button. Bend the two ends forward for the claws of the crab and trim off any extra. Put a tiny piece of masking tape on top of the crab to create a better gluing surface. Glue on two small black beads for eyes. Tuck the crab in among the grass seaweed at the bottom of the container.

5 Use a four-hole button to make each fish. Push a 2-inch (5-cm) piece of pipe cleaner through a hole in the button and fold it in on each side to form fins. Thread a second 2-inch piece through another hole and bend toward the back to make a tail. Put a tiny piece of masking tape on each side of the fish to create a better gluing surface for the wiggle eyes. Glue a tiny wiggle eye on each side of the fish.

6 Cut a 5-inch (13-cm) length of thread. Thread it through a top hole in the fish and tie it to the fish. Use cellophane tape to tape the ends of the thread to the inside of the lid so that, when it is put on the container, the fish hangs down freely, not touching the bottom of the container. Trim off any extra thread. You might want to make more than one fish.

Snap the lid on the container, and your ocean scene is ready to display.

Thank you, God, for all the creatures you put in the waters.

God made lots of little things
that creep, crawl, and fly.

Caterpillar on a Leaf

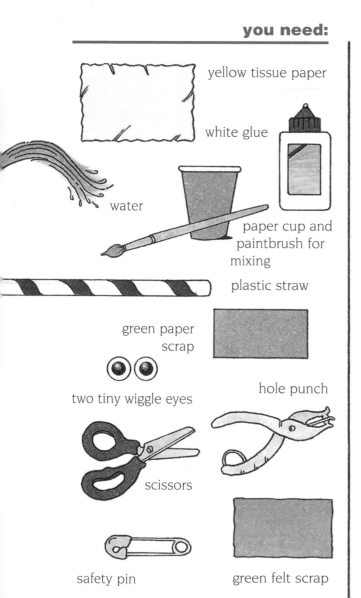

you need:

yellow tissue paper

white glue

water

paper cup and paintbrush for mixing

plastic straw

green paper scrap

two tiny wiggle eyes

hole punch

scissors

safety pin

green felt scrap

Styrofoam tray for drying

what you do:

1 Cut a strip of tissue paper 7 inches (18 cm) long and 2 inches (5 cm) wide.

2 Mix a small amount of glue with the same amount of water in the paper cup.

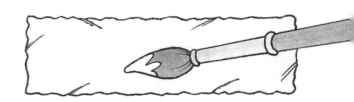

3 Working on the Styrofoam tray, use the paintbrush to cover the strip of tissue with watery glue. Roll the wet tissue around the plastic straw. Carefully slide the tissue paper together along the straw to make the segments of the caterpillar. Work from both ends of the tissue paper until the paper caterpillar is about 11/2 inches (3.75 cm) long.

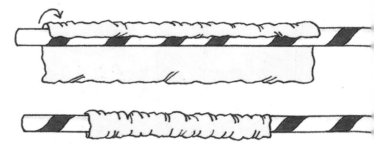

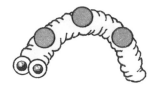

4 Carefully slide the caterpillar off the straw and snap it in the position you want it to dry. Let it dry completely on the Styrofoam tray. It will be hard when it dries.

5 Punch circles from the green paper. Glue the circles along the back of the caterpillar for spots. Glue two tiny wiggle eyes to one end of the caterpillar.

6 Cut a leaf shape from the green felt. Glue the caterpillar to the leaf shape.

You can display the caterpillar flat or add a safety pin to wear it as a lapel pin.

Thank you, God, for tiny things
that creep and crawl.

God made the animals.

Button Animals

what you do:

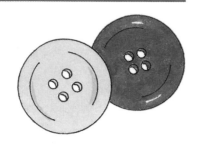

1-inch (2.5-cm) craft
buttons with four holes

pipe cleaner

tiny wiggle eyes

scissors

1 String a piece of pipe cleaner through one of the top holes of the button for the neck and head of the animal. Make the piece twice as long as you want the neck and head to be. String the piece halfway through and twist the two pieces together to form the neck. It might be an animal with a very long neck like a giraffe, or with a short neck like a cat. Fold the ends of the pipe cleaner down and back for the head, then tip the ends up for ears.

2 String a piece through the top back hole for a tail. Make the piece twice as long as you want the tail to be. Thread it halfway through the hole, then twist the two ends together around the button.

3 Cut two pieces of pipe cleaner for legs. Thread one piece through each hole, then twist the two ends around each other once below the button. Spread the two ends out to form a leg on each side of the button.

4 Glue two tiny wiggle eyes to the head of the button animal.

Make lots of different kinds of animals using different color buttons and pipe cleaners.

Thank you, God, for the animals.

God made all
the people.

Row of People

you need:

cardboard egg carton

poster paints in six bright
colors and a paintbrush

poster paints in
six skin tones

12 beads and/or
wiggle eyes

six tiny pom-poms

white
glue

red marker

buttons

yarn bits in
different hair
colors

six 12-inch (30-cm) pipe cleaners

ribbon for bow

masking
tape

scissors

newspaper
to work on

what you do:

1 Cut the lid off the top of the egg
carton. Paint the outside of the lid
for the "people" to sit on.

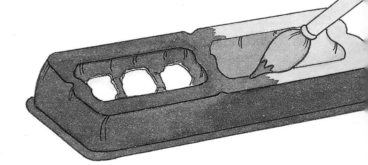

2 Turn the bottom part of the egg carton over. The top row of bumps will
be the heads for the people, and the bottom row the bodies. Paint each bump in
the top row a different skin tone. Paint
each bump in the bottom row a different
bright color.

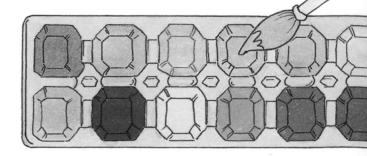

3 Glue two wiggle eyes or beads on each face. Glue on a pom-pom below each pair of eyes for the nose. Use the red marker to give each person a smile. Glue different color yarn bits on the top of each head for hair.

4 Decorate each body by gluing on a bow or button.

5 Fold each of the six pipe cleaners in half to form legs. Bend the ends to make feet. Glue the folded ends of the pipe-cleaner legs along the lid of the egg carton. Use masking tape to hold the legs in place while the glue is drying. Bend the legs down over the front of the carton to make knees.

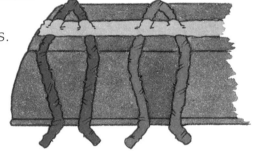

6 Glue the people across the lid of the carton over the legs so that each person has a pair of legs sticking out from the body.

Isn't it amazing how different each person is?

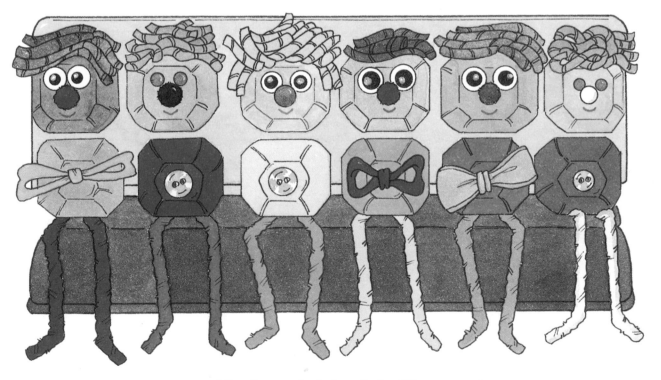

Thank you, God, for all the different people.

God made so many
different people!

Different People
Envelopes Puzzle

you need:

eight or more used white
envelopes with nothing
written on the back

what you do:

1 Line up four different envelopes, unwritten-on side
up, one below the other. Draw a head on the top
envelope. On the second envelope draw the upper body,
as a continuation of
the first drawing. On
the third envelope
draw the lower body
portion in pants or a
skirt. On the last
envelope draw the
legs and feet.

2 Remove the head envelope and replace it with a fresh one. Draw a different head on this one, but make it line up with the upper body below it. Do the same thing with each of the other envelopes. You can make as many different envelope pieces as you want, making sure each piece lines up with the original drawing.

3 Add details and color all the different parts with markers.

Have fun making lots of different-looking people by trying different combinations of envelope parts.

Thank you, God, for making each of us in your image.

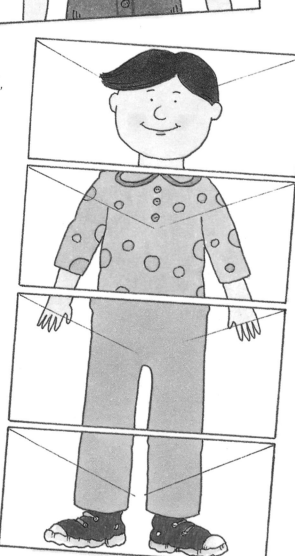

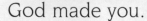

God made you.

Label Necklace

you need:

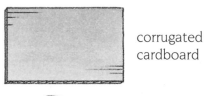

corrugated cardboard

scissors

markers

stickers

colored vinyl electrical tape

thin ribbon or yarn

hole punch

what you do:

1 Cut a 5- by 7-inch (13- by 18-cm) piece of corrugated cardboard. Snip off the corners at one end to make it look like a tag. Round off all the corners.

2 Use the markers to write, "Made with love by GOD" on one side of the tag. Decorate the tag any way you want using markers and stickers.

3 Use the electrical tape to make a border for the tag.

4 Punch a hole in the center of the end of the tag with the trimmed corners.

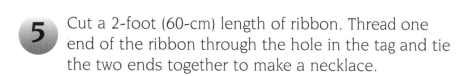

5 Cut a 2-foot (60-cm) length of ribbon. Thread one end of the ribbon through the hole in the tag and tie the two ends together to make a necklace.

You can wear the label as a reminder that you come from God.

Thank you, God, for making me.

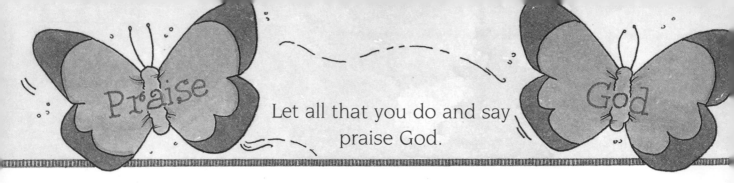

Let all that you do and say praise God.

Praise Puppet

you need:

plastic flip-top cap (found on salad dressing and shampoo bottles)

masking tape

white glue

scissors

red construction paper scrap

two wiggle eyes

tiny pom-pom

2-inch (5-cm) pom-pom

markers

what you do:

1 Turn the cap upside-down. The top of the cap will form the bottom jaw of the puppet. Cover the outside of the cap with masking tape. You can use the masking tape shade for the skin color, or use markers to make the skin another color.

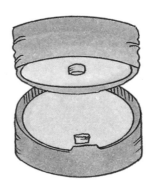

2 Trace around the cap on the red paper. Cut the circle out. Use a marker to write "Praise God" on the circle. Put a piece of masking tape on the inside of the bottom jaw to create a better gluing surface. Glue the circle inside the mouth of the puppet.

3 Use a marker to draw a smile on the bottom center of the jaw.

4 Put a tiny square of masking tape on the back of each wiggle eye to create a better gluing surface. Glue the eyes to the face, above the open mouth. Glue the tiny pom-pom just below the eyes for the nose.

5 Put a strip or two of masking tape inside the cap, again to create a better gluing surface.

6 Glue one side of the large pom-pom in the cap with most of it sticking out for hair.

This little puppet speaks only to praise God!

God, I praise your name forever and ever. Amen

Celebrating the Birth of Jesus . . .

Christians celebrate the birth of Jesus in so many ways.
NATIVITY PANELS 42

*Advent is the time before Christmas when preparations
are made to celebrate Jesus' birthday.*
ANGEL ADVENT CALENDAR 44

*Jesus' first bed was a manger, because He was
born in a stable in Bethlehem.*
CARDBOARD TUBE MANGER 46

*The three kings found the baby Jesus
by following a bright star.*
THREE KINGS HATS 48

Christmas is a time to cook special treats.
MAGI RECIPE HOLDER 50

We read about the events leading up to the birth of Jesus.
BIBLE ORNAMENT 52

*Greeting cards from families and friends are
a welcome part of the Christmas celebration.*
JOYFUL CARD HOLDER 54

People sing about the coming of Jesus.
JOY TO THE WORLD MAGNET 56

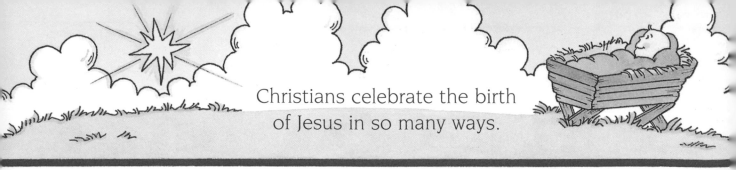

Christians celebrate the birth
of Jesus in so many ways.

Nativity Panels

you need:

cardboard

blue
glue
gel

scissors

ruler

plastic tape

gold glitter

gold spray paint

old
jewelry

Christmas
cards with scenes
of the Christmas story

newspaper
to work on

what you do:

1 Cut an arched window shape from the
cardboard about 1 foot (30 cm) tall and
8 inches (20 cm) wide.

2 Cut two sidepieces from the cardboard,
each about 8 inches square. Round off
the outer corners of the two squares.

3 Cover the edges of all three pieces with
the plastic tape.

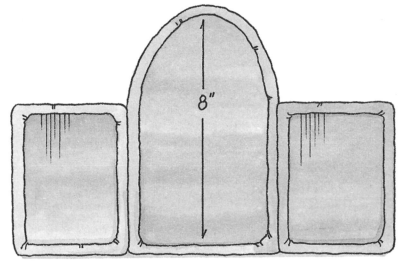

4 Attach the two sidepieces to each side
of the center unit with a strip of plastic
tape down the back seam of each piece. This
will allow the two sidepieces to swing forward to stand the triptych up.

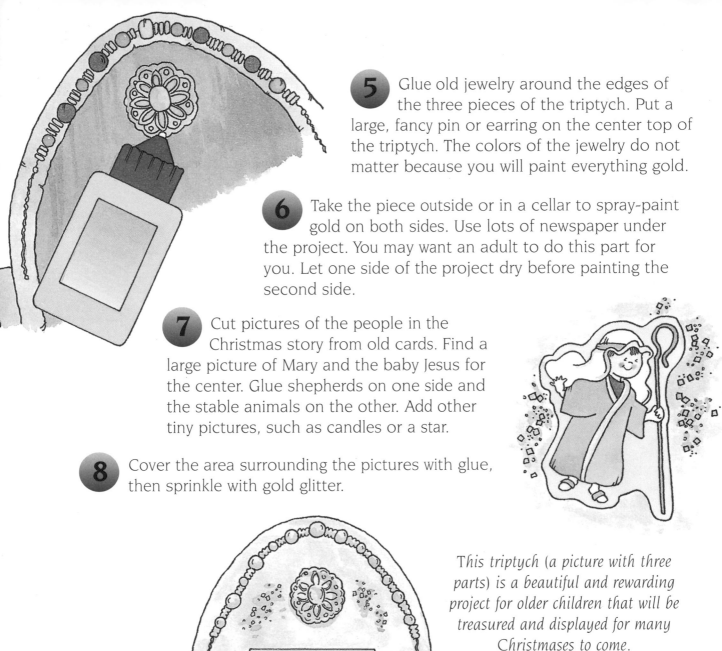

5 Glue old jewelry around the edges of the three pieces of the triptych. Put a large, fancy pin or earring on the center top of the triptych. The colors of the jewelry do not matter because you will paint everything gold.

6 Take the piece outside or in a cellar to spray-paint gold on both sides. Use lots of newspaper under the project. You may want an adult to do this part for you. Let one side of the project dry before painting the second side.

7 Cut pictures of the people in the Christmas story from old cards. Find a large picture of Mary and the baby Jesus for the center. Glue shepherds on one side and the stable animals on the other. Add other tiny pictures, such as candles or a star.

8 Cover the area surrounding the pictures with glue, then sprinkle with gold glitter.

This triptych (a picture with three parts) is a beautiful and rewarding project for older children that will be treasured and displayed for many Christmases to come.

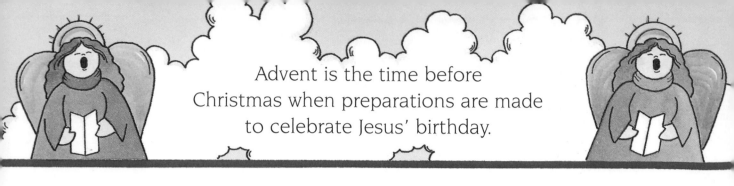

Advent is the time before
Christmas when preparations are made
to celebrate Jesus' birthday.

Angel Advent Calendar

you need:

4-inch (10-cm) square note pad with a gummed edge holding it together

yellow and skin-tone construction paper

white glue

scissors

markers

silver or gold sparkle stem

pen

thin ribbon

ruler

yarn in hair color of your choice

what you do:

1 Tear off a portion of the pad of paper with enough pages so that there will be one page for each day from the start of Advent until Christmas Eve. Advent begins on the first of the four Sundays before Christmas. Make sure you keep the pages held together by keeping the portion of the gummed binding that holds the pages together intact when you remove the stack of paper from the pad.

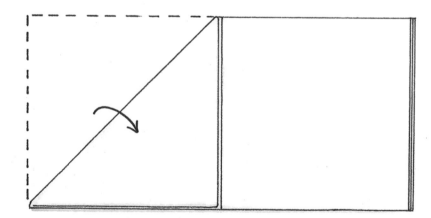

2 With the binding on the left, open the first page of the pad like a book. Fold the top corner down to the bottom corner to make each square a triangle. Fold each page this way except for the last one. Fold the last page so that the fold is inside the book, not outside. Fan the folded pages out and stand the pages up to form the dress for the angel.

3 Cut a 2-inch (5-cm) circle for the head of the angel. Use the markers to give the angel a face. Glue on yarn bits for hair. Shape her halo from a 4-inch (10-cm) piece of the sparkle stem. Glue the halo on top of the head. Glue the bottom edge of the head to the back, top of the dress.

4 Fold a piece of the yellow paper in half. Cut a wing shape on the fold. Open the folded paper to get two wings attached at the center. Glue the wings to the back of the angel.

5 Cut a 6-inch (15-cm) length of the ribbon. Tie the ribbon into a bow. Glue the bow to the dress under the angel's chin.

Unfold each page of the angel dress and write down something special to do that day to prepare for the birthday of Jesus. It could be something like reading the Christmas story, arranging your doll friends to make a nativity scene, praying, or making cards or gifts.

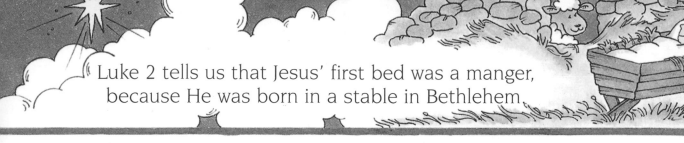

Luke 2 tells us that Jesus' first bed was a manger, because He was born in a stable in Bethlehem.

Cardboard Tube Manger

you need:

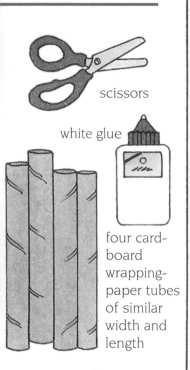

scissors

white glue

four cardboard wrapping-paper tubes of similar width and length

twine

large sheet of brown poster board

newspaper to work on

what you do:

1 Glue two of the cardboard tubes together in an X shape, with the centers crossing over each other. Glue the second pair of tubes in an X shape that exactly matches the first set of tubes. These will be the legs of the manger.

2 When the glue has dried, wrap twine around the meeting point of the two tubes of each leg to give the legs a rustic look. Trim off any extra and slip the end under the twine layers and tie it to keep it in place.

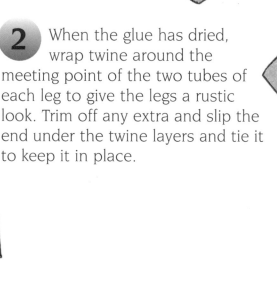

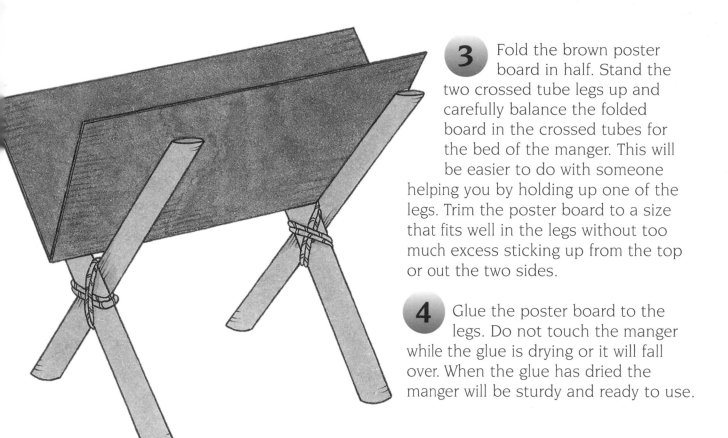

3 Fold the brown poster board in half. Stand the two crossed tube legs up and carefully balance the folded board in the crossed tubes for the bed of the manger. This will be easier to do with someone helping you by holding up one of the legs. Trim the poster board to a size that fits well in the legs without too much excess sticking up from the top or out the two sides.

4 Glue the poster board to the legs. Do not touch the manger while the glue is drying or it will fall over. When the glue has dried the manger will be sturdy and ready to use.

You might want to put some yellow yarn in the manger for hay and wrap up a baby doll to be the baby Jesus. The manger not only makes a pretty reminder of whose birthday we celebrate at Christmas, but it can also be used to play with as you act out the Christmas story.

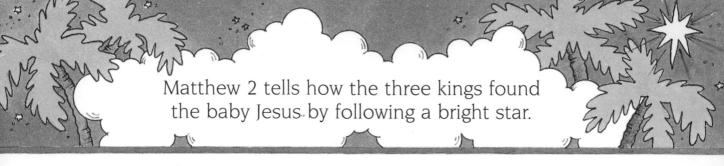

Matthew 2 tells how the three kings found the baby Jesus by following a bright star.

Three Kings Hats

you need:

poster paint in three different skin colors

paintbrush

white glue

scissors

black and brown yarn

sparkle stems

six wiggle eyes

small beads

three solid-colored foil party hats (or paint three printed hats)

large and small pom-poms in two different colors

cotton balls

masking tape

three 2 1/2-inch (6.3-cm) Styrofoam balls

foil doilies

three gold-colored buttons or earrings

ribbon, rickrack, and other trims

newspaper to work on

what you do:

1 Paint each of the three Styrofoam balls a different skin color. Let the paint dry.

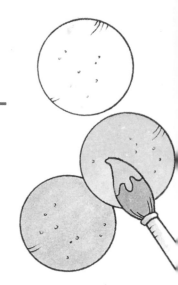

2 Press a head over the point of each hat. Slip the heads off again. Cover each point with glue and put the heads back on.

3 The hats will be the gowns of the kings. Decorate the gowns with pieces of the foil doilies and different trims. Make each king look different. For a gift, attach a gold button or earring to the front of each king, using a piece of rolled masking tape.

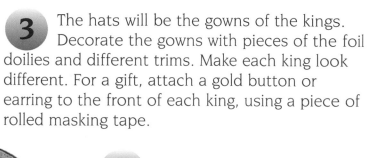

4 Glue on a pair of wiggle eyes for each king. Use the cotton and the black and brown yarn to give each king a different color hair and beard.

5 Use pieces of sparkle stem with beads strung on to make a crown for one of the kings. Use rickrack for another. Give the third king a hat by gluing the large pom-pom topped by the small pom-pom on top of his head.

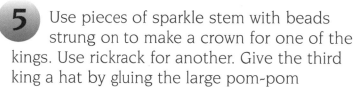

These kings look as good standing on a table as they do on your head.

Christmas is a time
to cook special treats.

Magi Recipe Holder

you need:

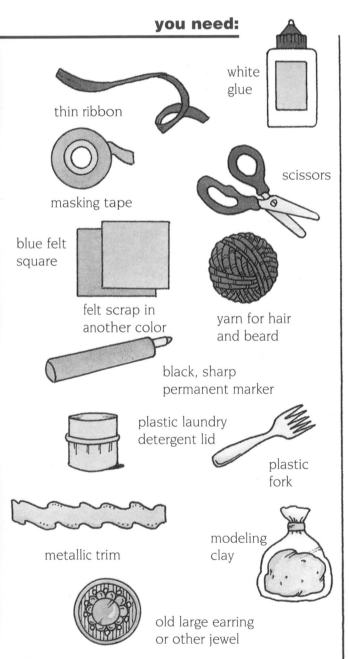

thin ribbon

masking tape

blue felt square

felt scrap in another color

black, sharp permanent marker

plastic laundry detergent lid

metallic trim

old large earring or other jewel

white glue

scissors

yarn for hair and beard

plastic fork

modeling clay

what you do:

1 Fill the plastic cap with modeling clay. Stand the handle of the fork in the clay so that it sticks straight up. The prongs of the fork will be the crown of the king and also serve as a holder for a recipe card.

2 Wrap the base of the fork with masking tape for the face of the king. Use the marker to draw the facial features on the tape on the bottom side of the fork.

3 Weave three rows of thin ribbon in and out through the prongs of the fork to form the base of the crown. Tie the two ends of the ribbon together when finished to hold it in place.

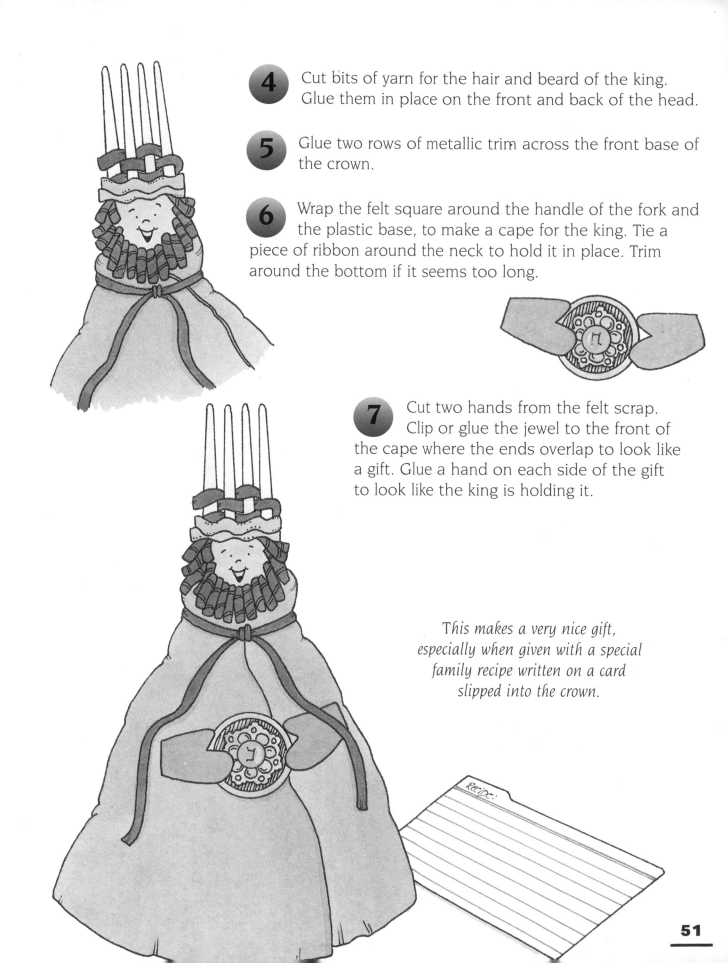

4 Cut bits of yarn for the hair and beard of the king. Glue them in place on the front and back of the head.

5 Glue two rows of metallic trim across the front base of the crown.

6 Wrap the felt square around the handle of the fork and the plastic base, to make a cape for the king. Tie a piece of ribbon around the neck to hold it in place. Trim around the bottom if it seems too long.

7 Cut two hands from the felt scrap. Clip or glue the jewel to the front of the cape where the ends overlap to look like a gift. Glue a hand on each side of the gift to look like the king is holding it.

This makes a very nice gift, especially when given with a special family recipe written on a card slipped into the crown.

Recipe:

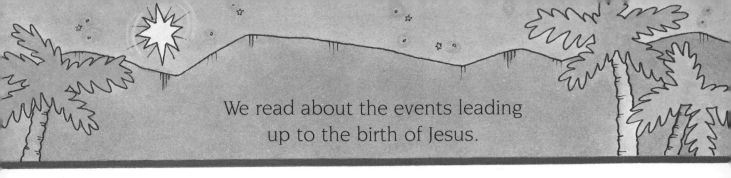

We read about the events leading
up to the birth of Jesus.

Bible Ornament

you need:

ruler

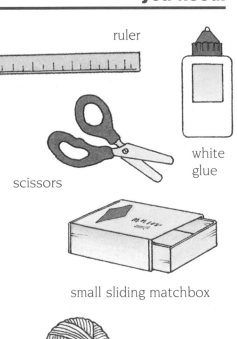

scissors

white
glue

small sliding matchbox

white string

black felt

pasta alphabet
letters

thin red ribbon

what you do:

1 To make the book
cover, cut one long side
out of the outer box of the
matchbox.

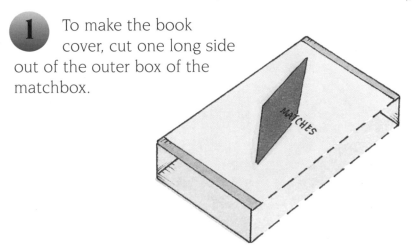

2 Cut a piece of black felt to cover the outer
piece and hang over the edge about 1/4
inch (0.5 cm). Round off the corners. Glue the felt
over the outer box to look like the black book
cover of a Bible.

3 Cut a 4-inch (10-cm) length of red ribbon. Glue the two ends into the top corner of the inner box with the loop of the ribbon sticking up for a hanger for the ornament.

4 Glue the inner box inside the outer cover.

5 Find the pasta letters to spell "Holy Bible." Glue the letters to the front cover of the book.

6 Cut 8 to 10 pieces of white string long enough to go around the three exposed edges of the inner box. Glue the strings, side by side, around the box edge to look like the pages of a book.

What a nice little reminder to read about the birth of Jesus.

Exchanging greeting cards is a welcome part of the Christmas celebration.

Joyful Card Holder

you need:

green plastic berry basket

two red 12-inch (30-cm) pipe cleaners

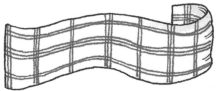

scissors

red plaid ribbon

eight jingle bells

what you do:

1 Cut out two opposite sides of the basket to remove them, leaving the corner supports intact. Cut the basket in half across the bottom. Overlap the two bottom pieces to make the card holder.

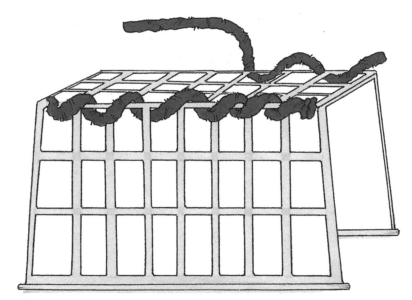

2 Cut the two pipe cleaners in half to get four pieces. Wind the end of one piece around one end of the bottom of one side of the holder. Weave the pipe cleaner in and out of the spaces on that side to sew the two pieces together. Wind the second end of the pipe cleaner around the basket to secure it. Do the same thing on the other side of the holder.

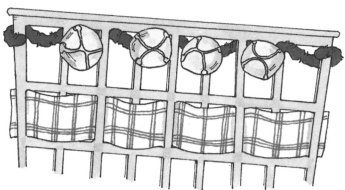

3 Weave a piece of ribbon through the open weave of the basket on each side of the holder. Trim the ends even with the sides of the holder.

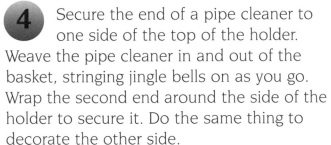

4 Secure the end of a pipe cleaner to one side of the top of the holder. Weave the pipe cleaner in and out of the basket, stringing jingle bells on as you go. Wrap the second end around the side of the holder to secure it. Do the same thing to decorate the other side.

This pretty card holder will work best when placed against a wall for extra support.

People sing about
the coming of Jesus.

Joy to the World Magnet

you need:

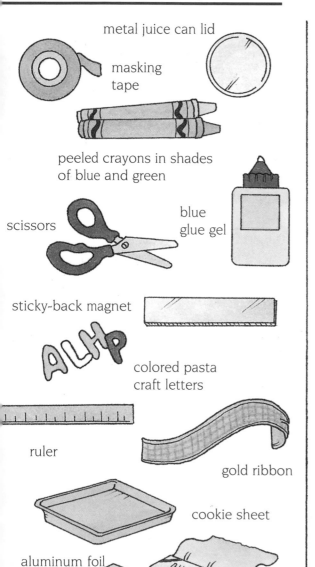

metal juice can lid

masking tape

peeled crayons in shades of blue and green

scissors

blue glue gel

sticky-back magnet

colored pasta craft letters

ruler

gold ribbon

cookie sheet

aluminum foil

blue or clear plastic wrap

what you do:

1 Cover the cookie sheet with foil to protect it. Put the lid on the foil and cover the lid with pieces of blue crayon. This will be the water on the earth. Put green crayon on top of the blue crayon at the center part of the lid to look like the land on the earth.

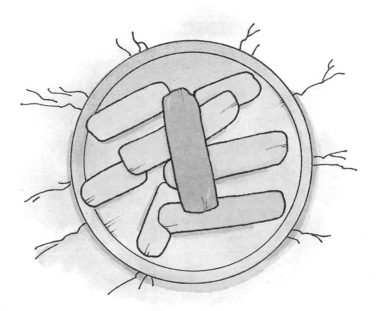

2 Ask a grown-up to put the lid in a 350-degree oven for two minutes to melt the crayon. After the grown-up removes the project from the oven, let it cool for a few minutes to harden.

3 Find the letters to spell "Joy to the World." Squeeze a line of glue gel on the front of the world for each word. Glue the letters in place. When the glue dries, the letters will not be stuck to the melted crayon background, but they will be stuck together to spell each word.

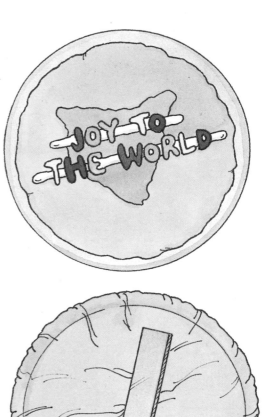

4 Arrange the words on the front of the world. Cut a 4-inch (10-cm) square of plastic wrap. Wrap the world tightly in the wrap to hold the words in place. Secure the wrap at the back of the world with masking tape and add the strip of sticky-back magnet, which will also help to hold the wrap in place.

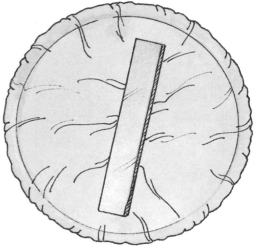

5 Put a tiny piece of masking tape at the top of the world. Cut an 8-inch (20-cm) length of ribbon. Tie the ribbon in a bow and trim the ends. Glue the bow to the top of the world.

"Joy to world, the Lord is come."

God has given us such a wonderful gift in his son, Jesus.

God's Gift

you need:

small jewelry gift box with a lid

ruler

cellophane tape

Christmas wrapping paper

Christmas tissue paper

white glue

small stick-on Christmas bow

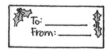
To: _____
From: _____
gift tag

Christmas card with nativity picture small enough to fit in box

scissors

what you do:

1 Wrap the lid of the box with the Christmas wrap just as you would a little package.

2 After "To:" on the gift tag write "The World." Cross out "From" and write "Love, God."

To: The World
From: Love, God

3 Glue the bow to the center top of the wrapped lid with the tag sticking out from under the bow.

4 Cut a 6-inch (15-cm) square of tissue paper. Glue the tissue in the box with the edges sticking out around the box. Trim the edges so that the tissue sticks out about 1 inch (2.5 cm) all around the box.

5 Cut the nativity scene from the Christmas card. Glue the scene to the bottom of the box.

6 Glue the lid of the box at an angle over the top left corner of the scene to look like a partly opened gift. When the glue has dried, stand this little reminder up on end for all to see.

What a wonderful gift!

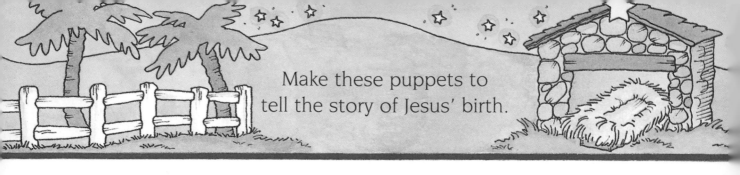

Make these puppets to
tell the story of Jesus' birth.

Spoon Puppets

you need:

(for each puppet)

plastic spoon

9- by 12-inch (23- by 30-cm) sheet of construction paper

construction paper scraps in skin tone of your choice

tissue paper

masking tape

ruler

markers

yarn for hair

scissors

white glue

clamp clothespins

thin ribbon

what you do:

1 Fold the sheet of construction paper lengthwise into a fan with 1-inch (2.5-cm) folds.

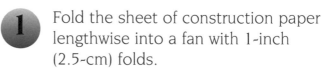

2 Cut a 3-inch (8-cm) slit down the center of the fan. Fold the two sides of the cut down on each side to form arms for the puppet and glue them to hold the fold. Use clamp clothespins to hold the paper in place while the glue dries.

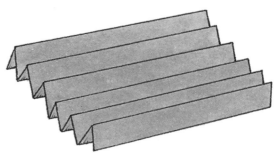

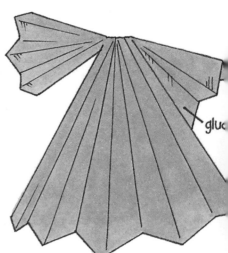

glue

3. Punch a hole through the two sides of the center-fold at the top of the dress, between the arms.

4. Cut a 1-foot (30-cm) length of ribbon. Thread an end of the ribbon through each hole from the back of the puppet and tie the ribbon in a bow.

5. Cut a 2-inch (5-cm) circle from the skin-tone paper scraps for the head. Use the markers to draw on a face. Glue on yarn bits for hair.

6. Cover the rounded back of the spoon with a piece of masking tape and glue the head to the spoon.

7. Slide the handle of the spoon through the ribbon at the neck of the dress, so the handle is behind the dress and the face is forward.

8. Give the figure a head covering by gluing on an 8-inch (20-cm) square of tissue.

To use the puppet, hold on to the handle of the spoon at the back. You can use this design to make all the adult figures in the Christmas story. Use different colors of paper, ribbon, and yarn for each figure. Make the baby Jesus by wrapping a wooden ice-cream spoon in white tissue, leaving the front of one end exposed to draw a face on with markers. You might want to glue the baby in the arms of the Mary puppet.

Christmas gives us
so many happy memories.

Christmas Memory Book

you need:

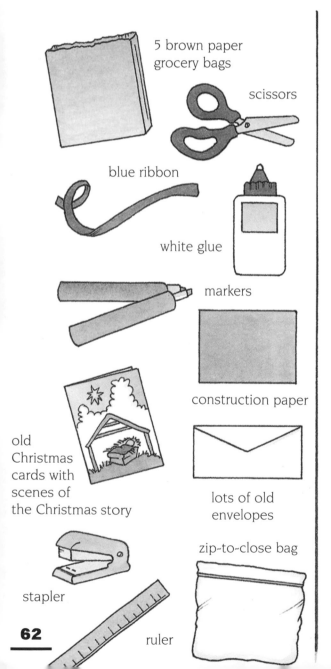

5 brown paper grocery bags

scissors

blue ribbon

white glue

markers

construction paper

old Christmas cards with scenes of the Christmas story

lots of old envelopes

zip-to-close bag

stapler

ruler

what you do:

1 Cut down the seam of each bag around the bottom to remove the bottoms from the bags.

2 Spread the cut bags out flat and stack them. Fold the stacked sheets in half to form a large book.

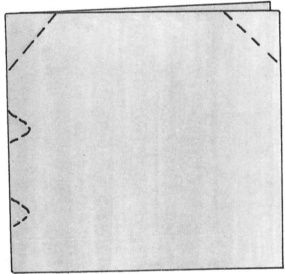

3 The front of the book will be decorated with a scene of the baby Jesus in the manger in the stable. Cut a 4-inch (10-cm) triangle off each corner at the top of the book to shape the roof of the stable.

4 Cut two small wedges out of the fold of the book.

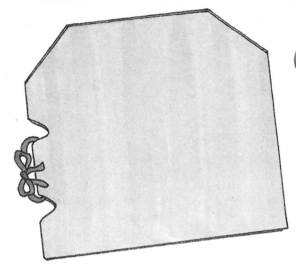

5 Cut two 6-inch (15-cm) pieces of ribbon. Thread a ribbon through each wedge-shaped hole and tie the ends in a bow to hold the book together.

6 Use markers, cut paper, and pieces cut from cards to make your own nativity scene on the front of the book. You might have some other ideas about how you want to make the scene.

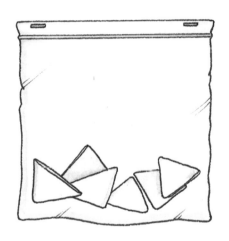

7 Cut 1-inch (2.5-cm) triangles off the bottom two corners of the envelopes. Put the clipped corners in a zip-to-close bag to save. Staple the back of the bag inside the back page of the book so that you can open the bag to get corners, then close it again to keep the extras from spilling out.

When you want to save a photo, card, program, or other item of paper in your book, slip an envelope corner on two opposite corners of the paper, or all four corners if you wish. Glue the back of the corners in the book to hold the paper in place without damaging it with tape or glue.

Fill your book with Christmas memories.

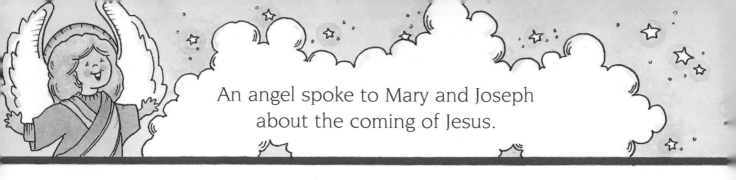

An angel spoke to Mary and Joseph about the coming of Jesus.

Ribbon Angel

you need:

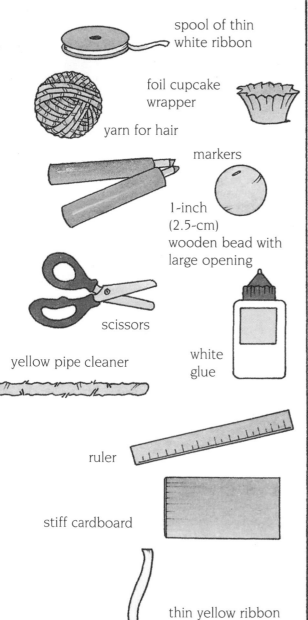

spool of thin white ribbon

foil cupcake wrapper

yarn for hair

markers

1-inch (2.5-cm) wooden bead with large opening

scissors

yellow pipe cleaner

white glue

ruler

stiff cardboard

thin yellow ribbon

what you do:

1 Cut a 4-inch (10-cm) square of cardboard. Wrap the white ribbon around the cardboard 20 times, then cut the end off from the spool.

2 Cut a 5-inch (13-cm) piece of ribbon. Thread the ribbon under the wrapped ribbon at one end of the cardboard. Tie the ribbon in a knot around the wrapped ribbon. Gather it together as tight as possible. Slip the ribbon off the cardboard.

3 Cut the front and back of the wrapped ribbon apart at the bottom to make the bottom of the dress of the angel. Trim the edge to even the ends of the ribbons out.

4 Wrap more white ribbon around the cardboard square 12 times for the arms.

5 Cut two 5-inch (13-cm) pieces of white ribbon. Slide the wrapped ribbon off the cardboard and tie each end with a piece of ribbon in a knot then a bow. Cut each end of the wrapped ribbon open to make hands.

6 Draw a face with the markers on the wooden bead. Glue on yarn bits for hair. Glue the folded end of the dress up inside the hole in the bottom of the bead head.

7 Slide the ribbon arms up in between the front and back ribbons of the dress. Cut a 5-inch (13-cm) piece of ribbon. Tie it around the dress below the arms to make the waist.

8 Fold the foil cupcake wrapper in half. Cut the folded wrapper in half to make two wings for the angel. Glue the two wings on the back of the angel sticking out from each side.

9 Shape a halo for the angel from the yellow pipe cleaner with a 1-inch (2.5-cm) piece sticking down from the halo. Glue the end of the halo down in the hole in the top of the bead head.

10 Cut a 5-inch (13-cm) piece of yellow ribbon. Tie the ribbon around the base of the halo then tie the two ends together to make a hanger for the angel.

You might want to try making angels in different colors.

Animals were part of
the Christmas story, too.

Camel Gift Bag

you need:

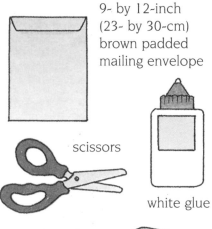

9- by 12-inch
(23- by 30-cm)
brown padded
mailing envelope

scissors

white glue

jingle bell

stapler

hole-punch

black marker

two shoulder
pads in colorful
prints

metallic ribbons
and trims

what you do:

1 Remove any labels from the side of the mailer.

2 Cut the top part of the bag off in a hump to form the top of the camel back.

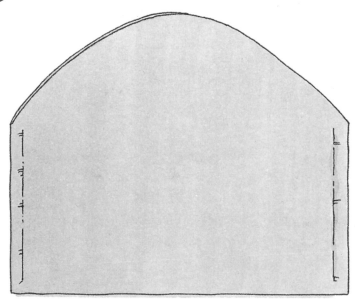

3 Cut a neck and head for the camel from the top part of the bag that was cut off.

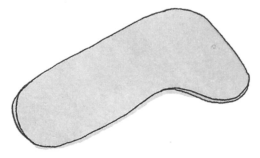

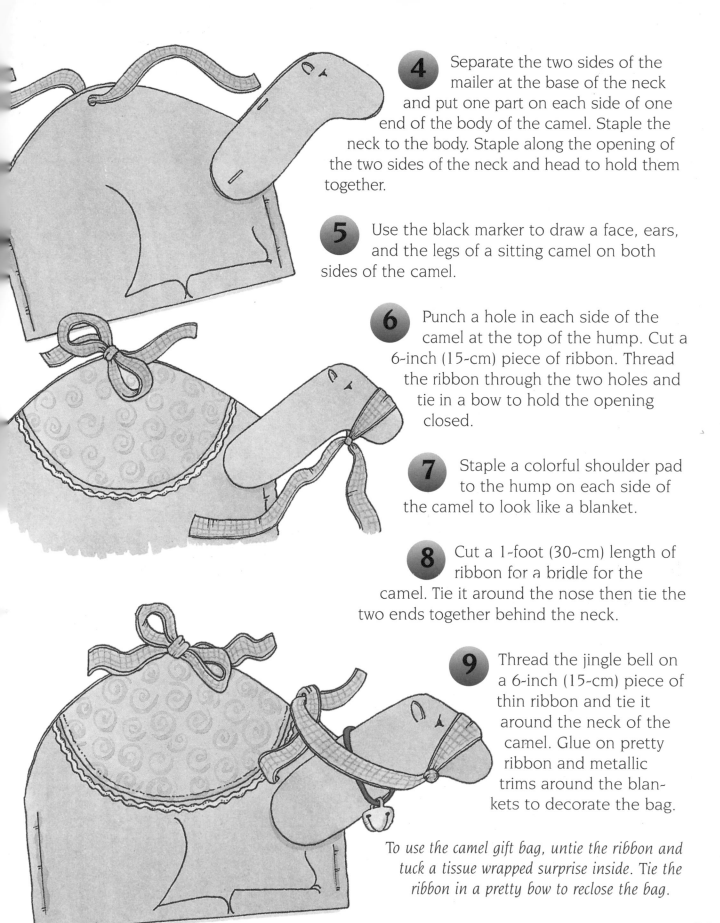

4 Separate the two sides of the mailer at the base of the neck and put one part on each side of one end of the body of the camel. Staple the neck to the body. Staple along the opening of the two sides of the neck and head to hold them together.

5 Use the black marker to draw a face, ears, and the legs of a sitting camel on both sides of the camel.

6 Punch a hole in each side of the camel at the top of the hump. Cut a 6-inch (15-cm) piece of ribbon. Thread the ribbon through the two holes and tie in a bow to hold the opening closed.

7 Staple a colorful shoulder pad to the hump on each side of the camel to look like a blanket.

8 Cut a 1-foot (30-cm) length of ribbon for a bridle for the camel. Tie it around the nose then tie the two ends together behind the neck.

9 Thread the jingle bell on a 6-inch (15-cm) piece of thin ribbon and tie it around the neck of the camel. Glue on pretty ribbon and metallic trims around the blankets to decorate the bag.

To use the camel gift bag, untie the ribbon and tuck a tissue wrapped surprise inside. Tie the ribbon in a pretty bow to reclose the bag.

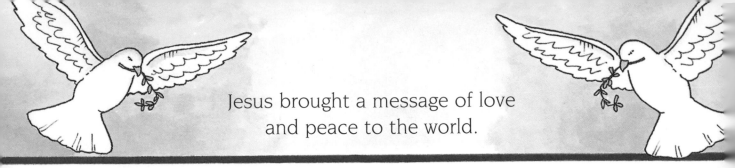

Jesus brought a message of love
and peace to the world.

Peaceful Dove Ornament

you need:

peanut

white glue

white poster
paint and a
paintbrush

plastic margarine
tub for mixing

clear
glitter

white and yellow
felt scraps

scissors

two blue
seed beads

Styrofoam tray
to work on

metallic thread

Christmas card with the
word "Peace" in the message

what you do:

1 Mix one part of white paint with
one part of glue in the margarine
tub. Paint the peanut white and immediately sprinkle with the clear glitter.

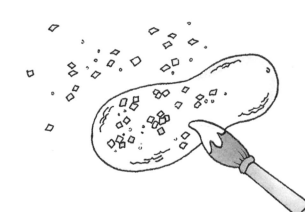

2 Fold the white felt in half and
cut a tiny wing for the dove on
the fold. Open the cut wing to get two
wings. Glue the part where the two
wings meet to the center of one side of
the peanut.

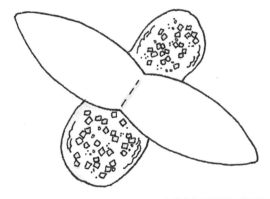

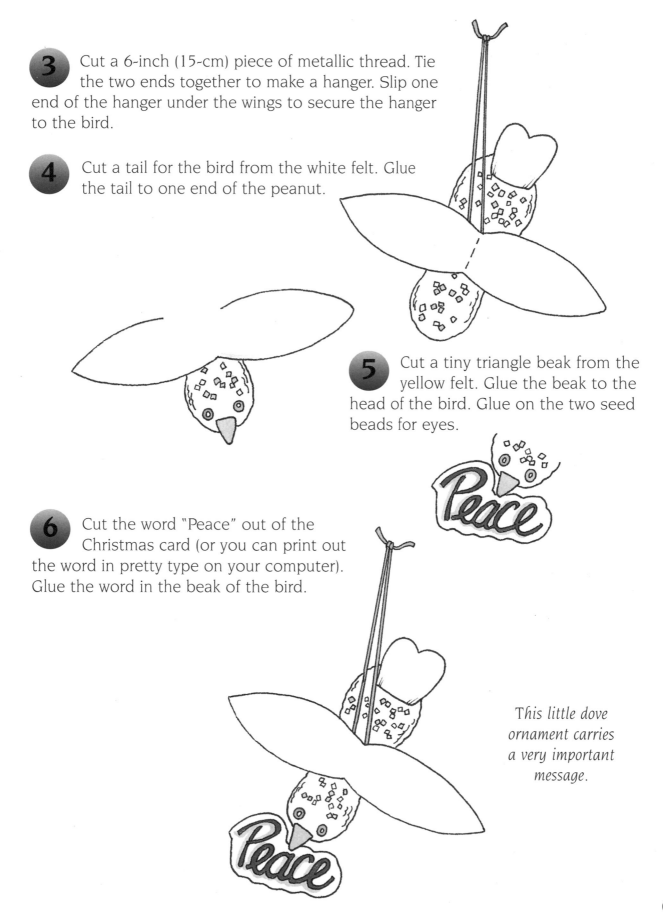

3 Cut a 6-inch (15-cm) piece of metallic thread. Tie the two ends together to make a hanger. Slip one end of the hanger under the wings to secure the hanger to the bird.

4 Cut a tail for the bird from the white felt. Glue the tail to one end of the peanut.

5 Cut a tiny triangle beak from the yellow felt. Glue the beak to the head of the bird. Glue on the two seed beads for eyes.

6 Cut the word "Peace" out of the Christmas card (or you can print out the word in pretty type on your computer). Glue the word in the beak of the bird.

This little dove ornament carries a very important message.

Christmas is the celebration of Jesus' birthday.

Happy Birthday, Jesus!

you need:

12- by 18-inch (30- by 46-cm) sheet of green construction paper

construction paper in your skin tone

roll of adding-machine tape

scissors

yarn in your hair color

white glue

9-inch (23-cm) uncoated paper plate

markers

white doily

ruler

white construction paper

what you do:

1 Fold the sheet of green construction paper in half lengthwise. Cut it apart on the fold.

2 Glue the two strips together to form one long strip for the arms.

3 Trace your hands on the skin-tone paper. Cut the two hand shapes out.

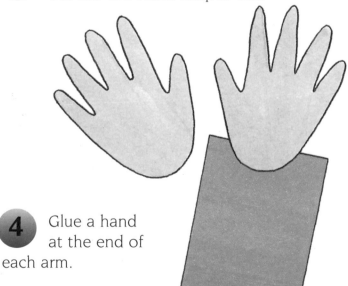

4 Glue a hand at the end of each arm.

5 From the white paper, cut cuffs for both sides of the arms and glue them on the end of each arm to cover the end of each hand.

6 Cut the doily in half. Glue the two halves to the center of the arms at an angle to make a collar.

7 Color the plate in your skin tone or leave it white. Draw on a face with the markers.

8 Cut yarn bits and glue them around the face for hair. If you are making a girl you might want to add a ribbon to the hair.

9 Glue the head to the top center of the arms with the collar under the chin portion of the paper-plate face.

10 Cut a 3-foot (90-cm) strip of adding-machine tape. Write "Happy Birthday Jesus" across the tape with markers. You might want to decorate the strip with designs or sticker stars.

11 Glue an end of the strip in each hand.

Fold the arms up to hide the paper strip. Open the arms wide to show the happy message.

This year, when you write your thank-you notes, write one to God, too.

Thank you for my family, for the blue skies.

Thank-You Note to God

you need:

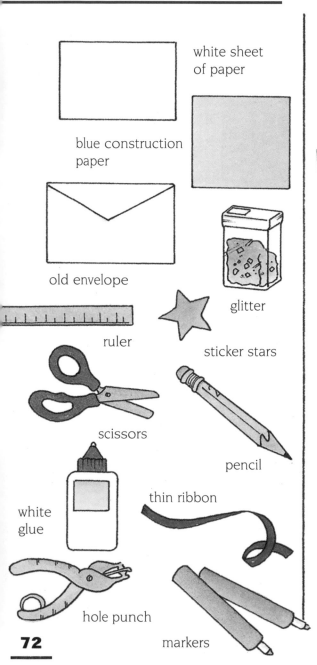

white sheet of paper

blue construction paper

old envelope

glitter

ruler

sticker stars

scissors

pencil

white glue

thin ribbon

hole punch

markers

what you do:

1 Carefully unglue the envelope to use as a pattern to make your own envelope. Trace around the envelope pattern on the blue paper. Cut the tracing out.

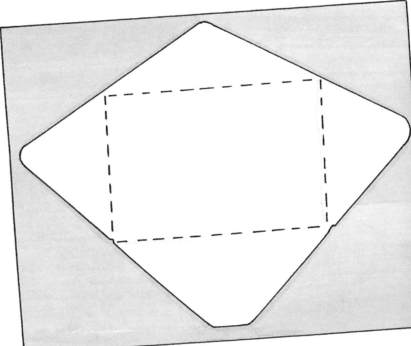

2 Fold the new envelope exactly like the one you used for a pattern. Use glue to hold the folds in place. Do not glue the envelope shut.

3 Write "To God" on the front of the envelope. On the back write "Christmas, 200_." Decorate the envelope with glitter and sticker stars.

4 On the white sheet of paper, write a letter to God that says thank-you for all the gifts of the Christmas season. Remember all the special things that you did and the special people you did them with. End your letter by saying thank-you for the gift of Jesus.

5 Fold the letter and put it in the pretty envelope you made.

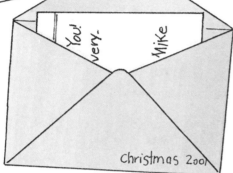

6 Punch a hole in the corner of the envelope. Cut a 6-inch (15-cm) piece of ribbon. String one end of the ribbon through the hole then tie the ends together to make a hanger.

Write a thank-you note to God each Christmas. Keep the letters with your Christmas things to hang on the tree each year. Fill your tree with a lifetime of thank-you notes to God.

Our Favorite Bible Stories

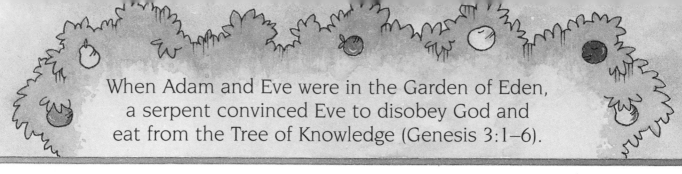

When Adam and Eve were in the Garden of Eden, a serpent convinced Eve to disobey God and eat from the Tree of Knowledge (Genesis 3:1–6).

The Tree of Knowledge

you need:

four 12-inch (30-cm) brown pipe cleaners

scissors

scrap of orange paper

ruler

12 small red beads

one 12-inch (30-cm) green pipe cleaner or sparkle stem

white glue

green yarn

Styrofoam tray to work on

green poster paint and a paintbrush

cardboard egg carton

black sharp-pointed marker

what you do:

1 Fold three of the brown pipe cleaners in half. Twist them together above the folded ends to form a tree trunk, with the ends of the pipe cleaners fanning out to form the branches of the tree. Cut the last brown pipe cleaner into 1-inch (2.5-cm) pieces. Wrap the pieces around the branches of the tree to make smaller branches.

2 Slip the beads onto the branches to look like apples on the tree.

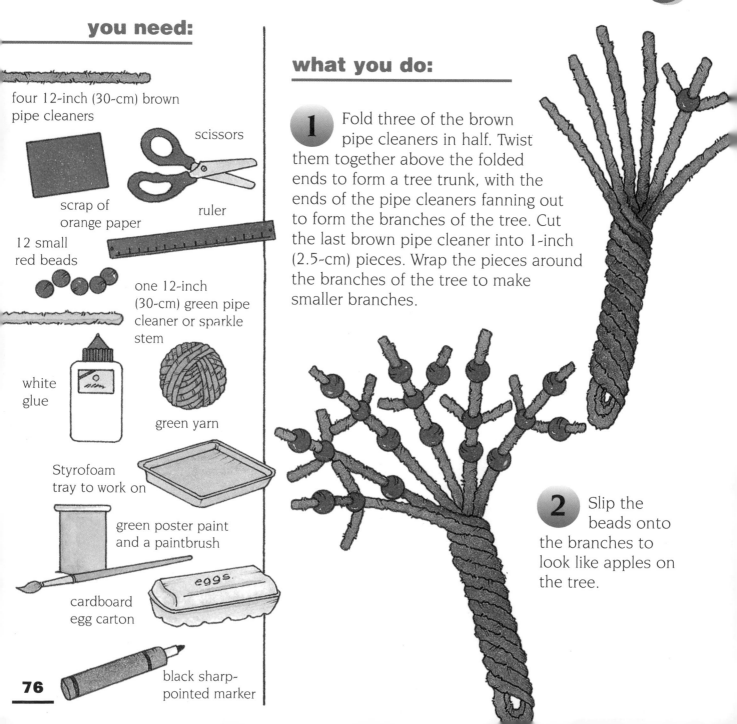

3 Wrap the branches of the tree with green yarn to look like the leaves. Tie one end of a long piece of yarn to a branch, then weave it in and out through the branches until the branches are all entwined. When you like the way the tree looks, trim off any extra yarn and tie the end to a branch to secure it. If you feel your first piece of yarn wasn't long enough to cover the branches well, just tie on another piece.

4 Cut a cup from the cardboard egg carton and paint it green. Let it dry. Turn the cup over and poke a hole in the center to slip the base of the tree through to make a stand for the tree.

5 Wrap the green sparkle stem around the base of the tree to look like the serpent. Cut two tiny eyes for the serpent from the orange paper scrap. Use the black marker to put a pupil in the center of each eye. Glue the eyes to the end of the green sparkle stem.

The serpent in the Tree of Knowledge reminds us that there are sometimes sad consequences of disobeying!

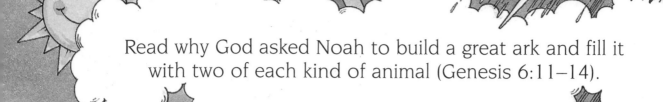

Read why God asked Noah to build a great ark and fill it with two of each kind of animal (Genesis 6:11–14).

Noah's Ark

you need:

two 9-inch (23-cm) uncoated paper plates

scissors

markers

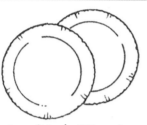

white glue

colored construction paper for animals

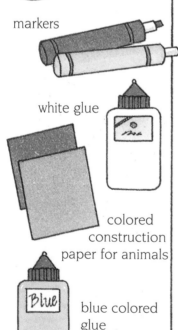

blue colored glue

paper fastener

what you do:

1 Fold one plate in half so that you know where the center is located. Cut the plate into two pieces about 1/2 inch (1.25 cm) off center so that one piece is about 1 inch (2.5 cm) bigger than the other piece.

2 Color the two pieces with the markers, then glue them together, eating sides in, to form the boat.

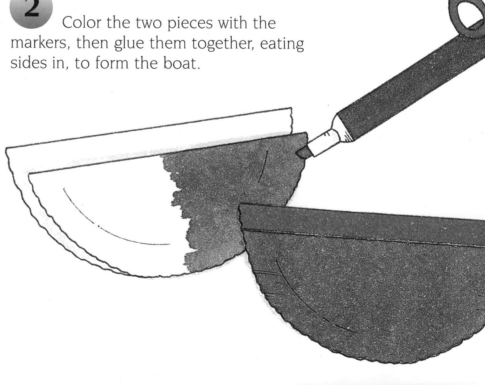
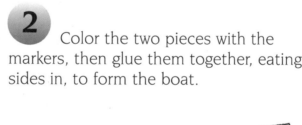

3 Cut animals from the construction paper to put in the ark. Don't forget to make two of each animal. Use markers to add details to the animals.

4 Draw a line across the center of the second paper plate. Use the markers to color a storm scene on one half of the plate. If you wish you can put raindrops on your storm scene using drops of blue glue. Turn the plate upside down and color a rainbow in a blue sky with a dove carrying an olive branch on the other half.

5 Use the paper fastener to attach the center of the boat to the center of the back plate.

Put your animals on board. To change the scene from the forty days of rain to the promise of dry land, turn the back plate around. God keeps His promises.

God keeps His promise to Abraham
and his wife Sarah and gives them a baby, Isaac,
in their old age (Genesis 18:9–10).

Sarah and Baby Isaac Puppet

you need:

scissors

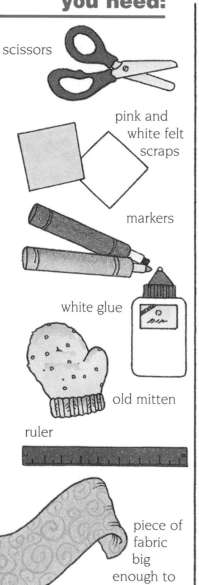

pink and white felt scraps

markers

white glue

old mitten

ruler

piece of fabric big enough to wrap around mitten

what you do:

1 From the pink felt, cut a circle for Sarah's face. Make the circle about as wide as the top of the mitten you are using. Draw a face on the felt circle using the markers. Glue the face to the top, palm side of the mitten.

2 Cut a tiny circle about as wide as the thumb of the mitten for the baby's face. Use the markers to draw on facial features. Glue the face to the top of the thumb of the mitten.

3 Cut a 3-inch (8-cm) triangle from the white felt for the baby's blanket. Wrap it around the thumb of the mitten with the baby's face peeking out. Glue the blanket in place.

4 Cut a rectangle of fabric large enough to wrap around the mitten and base of the thumb for Sarah's clothes. Wrap it around the mitten with the face peeking out and glue the fabric to the mitten.

To use the puppet slip your hand into the mitten and wiggle the little baby Isaac that Sarah is holding in her arms.

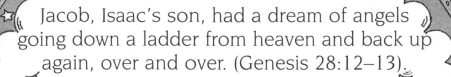

Jacob, Isaac's son, had a dream of angels going down a ladder from heaven and back up again, over and over. (Genesis 28:12–13).

Jacob's Ladder

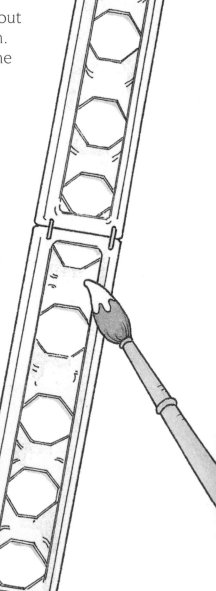

you need:

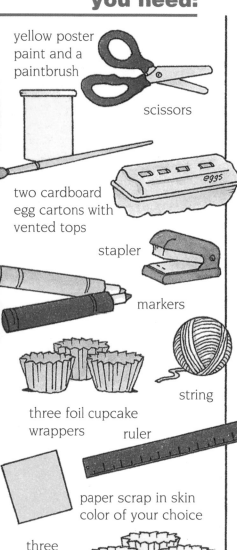

yellow poster paint and a paintbrush

scissors

two cardboard egg cartons with vented tops

stapler

markers

string

three foil cupcake wrappers

ruler

paper scrap in skin color of your choice

three yellow paper cupcake wrappers

newspaper to work on

what you do:

1 Cut the long vented center out of the lid of each egg carton. Staple the two strips together at the center to form a ladder.

2 Paint the ladder yellow and let it dry.

3 To make each angel, fold a foil cupcake wrapper in half, then fold the two sides back over each other to make a dress.

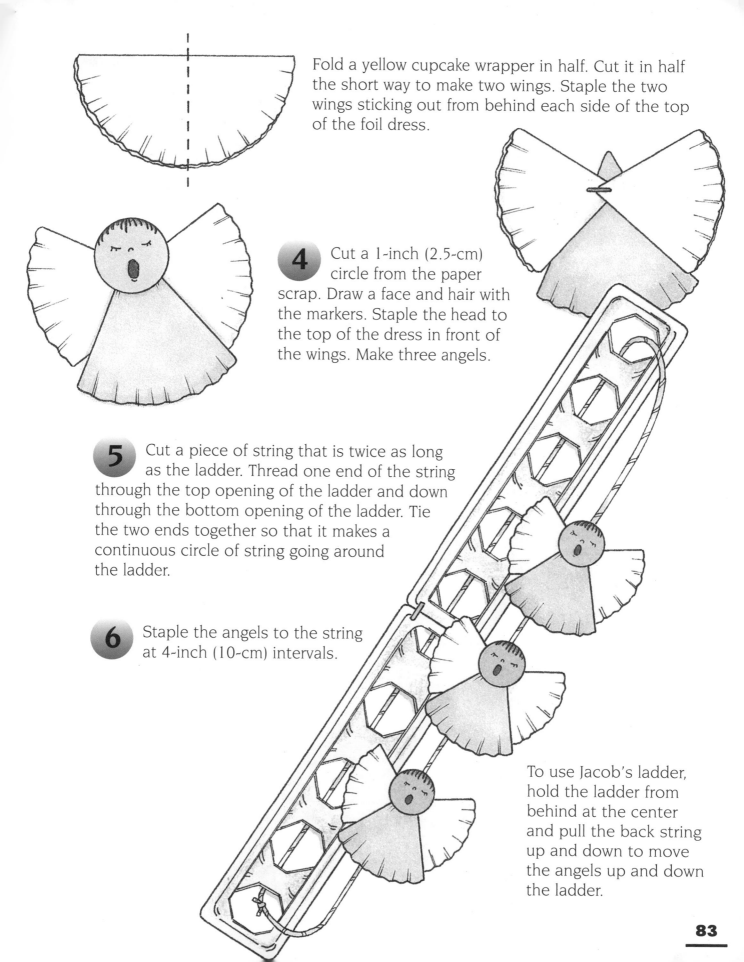

Fold a yellow cupcake wrapper in half. Cut it in half the short way to make two wings. Staple the two wings sticking out from behind each side of the top of the foil dress.

4 Cut a 1-inch (2.5-cm) circle from the paper scrap. Draw a face and hair with the markers. Staple the head to the top of the dress in front of the wings. Make three angels.

5 Cut a piece of string that is twice as long as the ladder. Thread one end of the string through the top opening of the ladder and down through the bottom opening of the ladder. Tie the two ends together so that it makes a continuous circle of string going around the ladder.

6 Staple the angels to the string at 4-inch (10-cm) intervals.

To use Jacob's ladder, hold the ladder from behind at the center and pull the back string up and down to move the angels up and down the ladder.

83

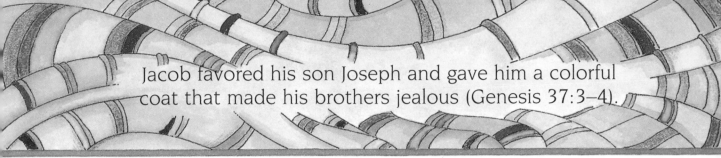

Jacob favored his son Joseph and gave him a colorful coat that made his brothers jealous (Genesis 37:3–4).

Joseph Magnet

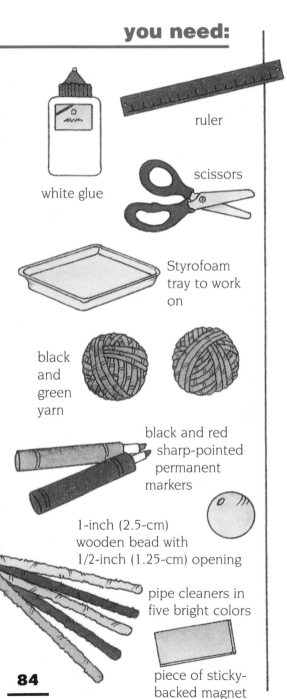

you need:

white glue

ruler

scissors

Styrofoam tray to work on

black and green yarn

black and red sharp-pointed permanent markers

1-inch (2.5-cm) wooden bead with 1/2-inch (1.25-cm) opening

pipe cleaners in five bright colors

piece of sticky-backed magnet

what you do:

1 Trim five different colored pipe cleaners to a length of 8 inches (20 cm). Bunch the pipe cleaners together and fold them in half. Dip the folded end in glue and stick it into the hole in the bead. The bead will be the head and the pipe cleaners the colorful coat. Trim the bottom of the pipe cleaners to even them out.

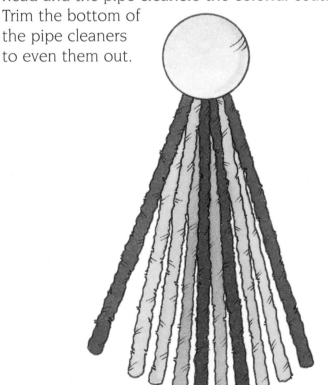

2 Cut one 3-inch (8-cm) piece from each of three different colored pipe cleaners for the sleeves of the coat. Slide them up between the pipe cleaners, forming the coat, and glue them in place. Tie a belt of green yarn around the coat just below the arms to help secure them.

3 Use the markers to draw a face on the bead. Glue on bits of black yarn for the hair.

4 Press a piece of sticky-backed magnet on the back of the pipe-cleaner coat and hang the project on your refrigerator.

Joseph is a wonderful reminder that even when things seem hopeless, God is there with a plan to make things right for us.

milk
dog bones
bread

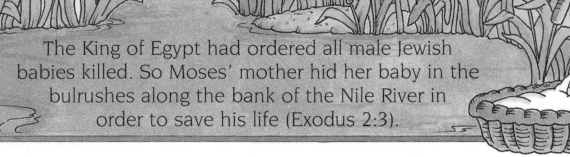

The King of Egypt had ordered all male Jewish babies killed. So Moses' mother hid her baby in the bulrushes along the bank of the Nile River in order to save his life (Exodus 2:3).

Moses in the Bulrushes Glove Puppet

you need:

scissors

cardboard egg carton

yellow poster paint

paintbrush

felt in blue, white, brown, and skin color

black yarn

white glue

two small wiggle eyes

old knit glove

newspaper to work on

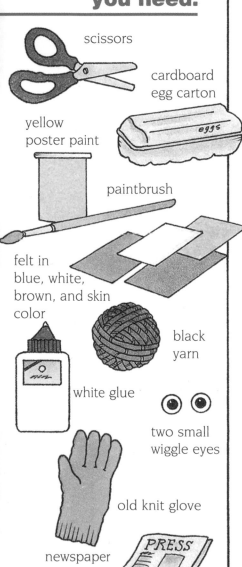

what you do:

1 Cut one egg cup from the egg carton. Cut a hole through one side of the bottom of the cup large enough to put your finger through. Paint the cup yellow and let it dry. This will be the basket for baby Moses.

2 From the blue felt, cut a pool of water that is wider than the glove. Cut a slit across the middle of the pool and slide it over the fingers and thumb of the glove so that the water surrounds them.

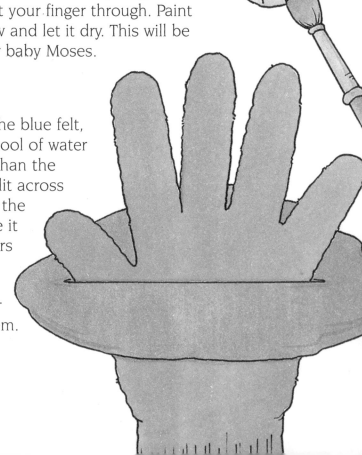

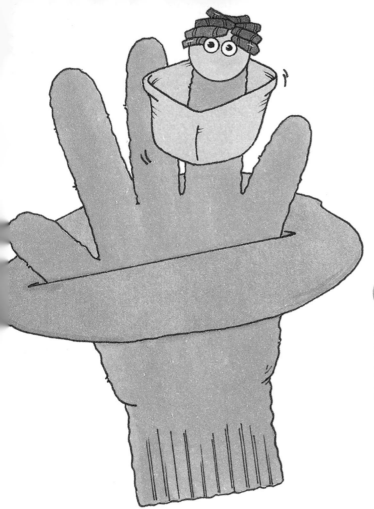

3 Slide the basket down over one of the middle fingers of the glove. Cut a 1-inch (2.5-cm) circle of skin-color felt for the head of the baby and glue it to the tip of the finger in the basket. Glue yarn bits to the top of the head for hair. Glue two wiggle eyes below the hair.

4 Cut a square of white felt for a blanket. Glue the blanket in the egg cup so that only the baby's eyes are peeking out.

5 Cut about seven long leaf shapes from the brown felt for the bulrushes that grew in the river. Glue them on the fingers and in the water so that the basket looks like it is floating among them.

To use the glove puppet put your hand in and wiggle your fingers to bob baby Moses up and down in the water among the bulrushes.

Among the many miracles God performed for His people was the parting of the waters of the Red Sea to let them escape from slavery (Exodus 14:26–27).

The Parting of the Red Sea

you need:

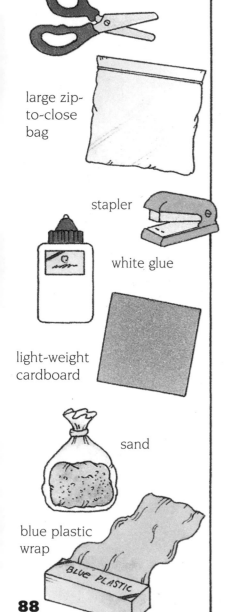

scissors

large zip-to-close bag

stapler

white glue

light-weight cardboard

sand

blue plastic wrap

what you do:

1 Carefully cut down the two sides of the zip-to-close bag and open it out flat.

2 Cut a square of light-weight cardboard that will fit exactly in the center of the flattened bag and allow the bag to fold up over each side of the cardboard and zip closed. Staple the cardboard to the plastic bag.

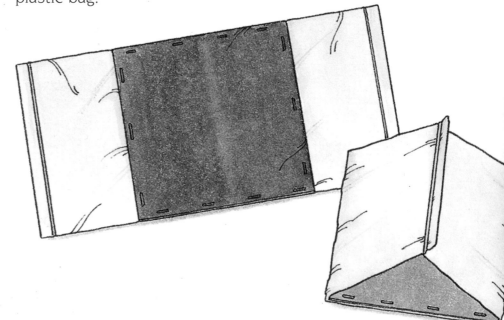

3 Cover the cardboard with glue, then sprinkle it with sand to look like the bottom of the sea. You may want to add some cut-out starfish or seashells.

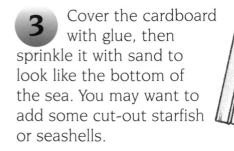

4 Crumble several squares of blue plastic wrap to fit over the flap of plastic bag on each side of the ocean bottom. Attach the crumbled pieces to the inside and outside of the bag flaps using a stapler to hold them in place. Use just enough pieces to cover the flaps. If you make it too thick the two flaps will no longer meet and close over the sandy bottom. Do not staple too close to the zipper.

Close the waters over the sandy bottom by zipping the two sides together. Show how the waters parted for Moses and the Israelites, then closed again once they were safely across.

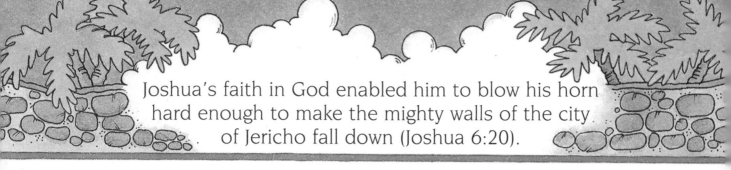

Joshua's faith in God enabled him to blow his horn hard enough to make the mighty walls of the city of Jericho fall down (Joshua 6:20).

Ram Horn Trumpet

you need:

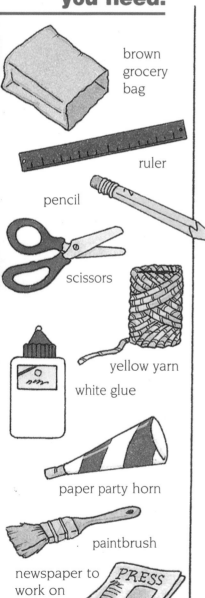

brown grocery bag

ruler

pencil

scissors

yellow yarn

white glue

paper party horn

paintbrush

newspaper to work on

what you do:

1 Cut a 12-inch (30-cm) square piece from the brown bag.

2 Use the paintbrush to spread white glue all over one side of the square.

3 Starting at one corner, roll the square around the party horn and into a cone shape, trimming off any excess.

4 Bend the wide end of the cone shape up about one-third of the way from the end. Let it dry completely to be sure the bent shape will hold.

5 Cut a 3-foot (90-cm) length of yarn and tie each end around the horn as shown so you can carry it over your shoulder.

Blow the horn and imagine you are helping to make the walls of Jericho fall down.

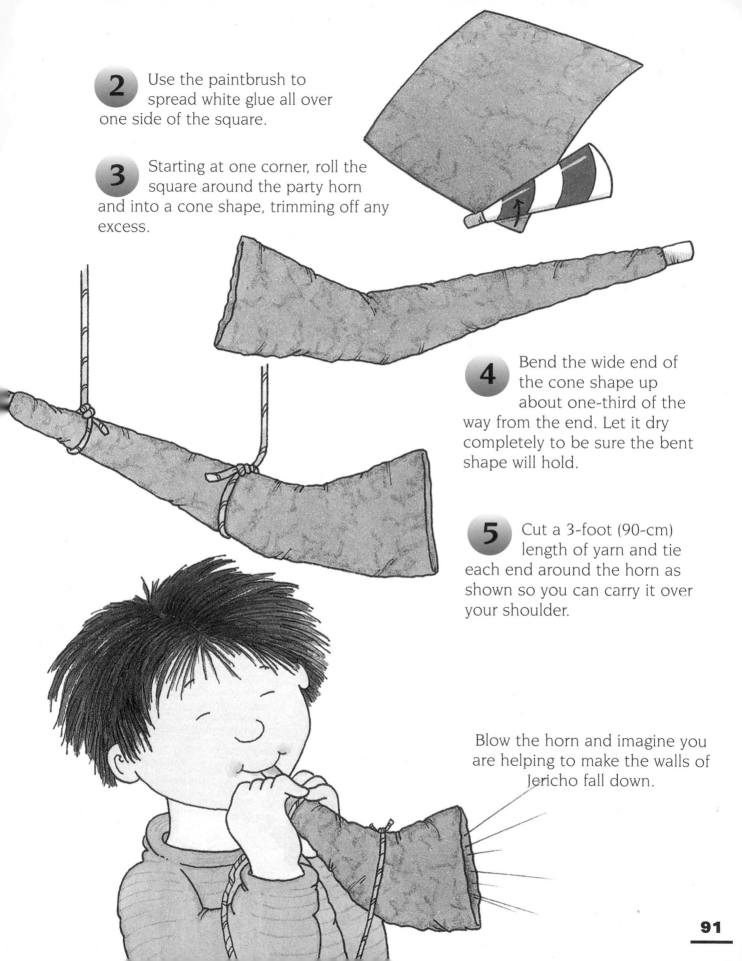

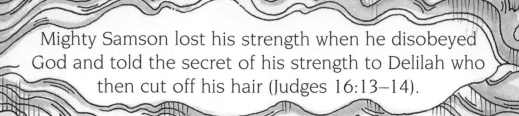

Mighty Samson lost his strength when he disobeyed God and told the secret of his strength to Delilah who then cut off his hair (Judges 16:13–14).

Hair-Growing Samson

you need:

pencil

construction paper in skin color

white glue

markers

cardboard toilet-tissue tube

scissors

cardboard egg carton

dirt

Styrofoam egg carton

grass seed

water

what you do:

1 Draw a body for Samson on the construction paper as tall as the cardboard tube. Do not draw a head on the body. Use the markers to draw on clothes. Cut out the body and glue it to one side of the cardboard tube.

2 Cut a cup from the cardboard egg carton for the head. Use markers to draw a face on one side of the head, with the open end of the cup up.

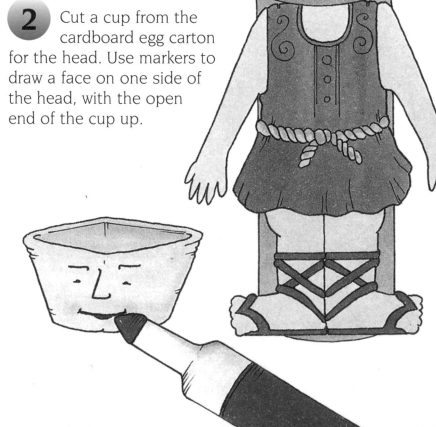

3 Glue the head to the top of the body.

4 Cut a cup from the Styrofoam egg carton. Put it inside the cardboard cup head for a liner.

5 Fill the head with dirt and sprinkle with grass seed. Don't forget to water the seed lightly every few days.

Can you put Samson in a sunny window and help him grow his hair back?

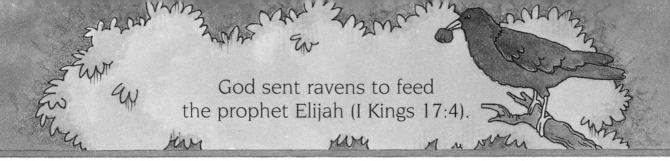

God sent ravens to feed
the prophet Elijah (I Kings 17:4).

Elijah and the Ravens Puppets

you need:

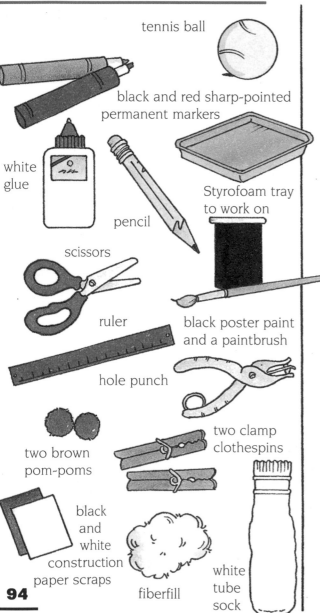

tennis ball

black and red sharp-pointed
permanent markers

white
glue

pencil

Styrofoam tray
to work on

scissors

ruler

black poster paint
and a paintbrush

hole punch

two brown
pom-poms

two clamp
clothespins

black
and
white
construction
paper scraps

fiberfill

white
tube
sock

what you do:

1 Ask a grown-up to cut a 2-inch (5-cm) slit across one side of the tennis ball for a mouth for the puppet. You will also need a 1-inch (2.5-cm) slit cut in the bottom side of the ball to attach the body of the puppet.

2 Use the red marker to draw lips around the puppet's mouth. Draw the rest of the face with the black marker.

3 Glue on hair and a beard made from fiberfill—or you can make a shorter beard from cotton.

4 Trim the cuff of the tube sock so that you are left with a sock about 11 inches (28 cm) long. Use the pencil to help you stuff the toe of the sock into the slit in the bottom of the ball.

5 Draw arms and other details of the robe with the black marker.

6 The two clothespins will be the ravens. Paint them black and let them dry on the Styrofoam tray.

7 Cut wings for each bird from the black paper. Glue the wings on one side of each clothespin.

8 Punch out two eyes for each bird from the white paper. Use the black marker to draw a dot in the middle of each eye for a pupil. Glue the eyes to the top bar of each clothespin toward the clamp end.

9 To feed Elijah, put a pom-pom in each raven's mouth to represent the bread and the meat sent to Elijah by God. Hold each side of the head and squeeze to make the mouth open. Fly each raven to Elijah and squeeze the back of the clothespin to release the food into Elijah's mouth.

God will take care of you, too.

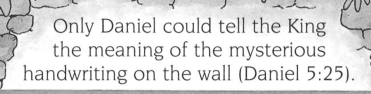

Only Daniel could tell the King
the meaning of the mysterious
handwriting on the wall (Daniel 5:25).

The Handwriting Appears on the Wall

you need:

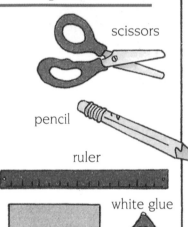

scissors

pencil

ruler

white glue

12- by 18-inch (30- by 46-cm) sheet of construction paper in wall color

marker

construction paper in skin color

what you do:

1 Cut a 3- by 18-inch (8- by 46-cm) strip off the bottom of the construction paper you are using for the wall.

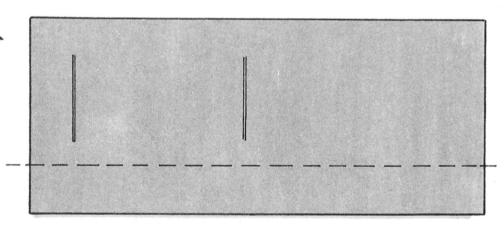

2 Cut a 4-inch (10-cm) slit up the middle of one side of the larger sheet of paper. Cut a parallel slit about 9 inches (23 cm) to the left of the first cut.

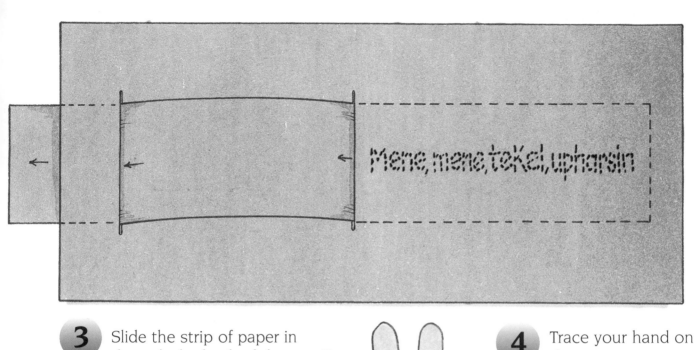

3 Slide the strip of paper in through the back of the middle cut, over the front of the paper, and through the cut on the edge. When the paper is exactly lined up behind the larger sheet, the wall should look blank. On the part of the paper that is hidden behind the larger paper write *Mene, mene, tekel, upharsin*, which was a warning to the evil king.

4 Trace your hand on the construction paper in the skin color. Cut out the hand outline. Glue the hand to the paper on the wall so that the fingers cover the center slit in the paper.

To make the hand look like it is writing a warning on the wall, slowly pull the smaller paper to one side to reveal the hidden message.

Jonah was thrown off a boat in a stormy sea and spent three long days in the belly of a big fish (Jonah 1:17).

Jonah in the Big Fish Puppet

you need:

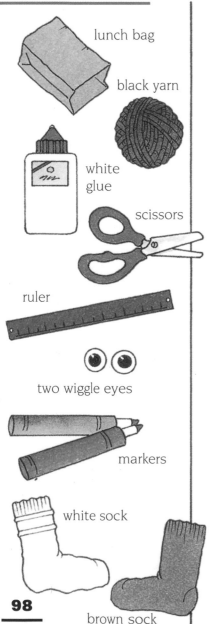

lunch bag

black yarn

white glue

scissors

ruler

two wiggle eyes

markers

white sock

brown sock

what you do:

1 To turn the lunch bag into a big fish cut a triangle out of the open end to form a tail. Cut an opening across the bottom of the bag and about 1 inch (2.5 cm) up each side to make the open mouth of the fish. Use markers to draw on eyes and any other details you might want to add.

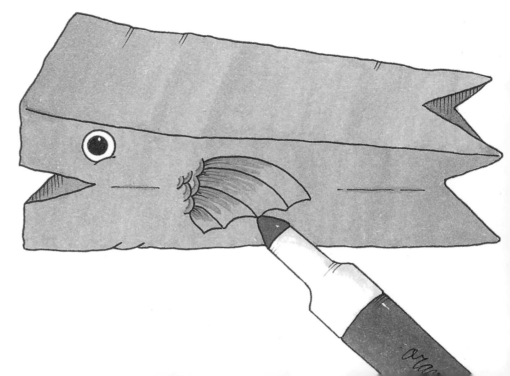

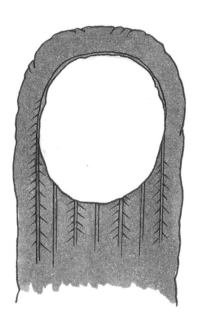

2 To make Jonah, cut a 2-inch (5-cm) circle out of the top of the toe of the brown sock. Put the white sock inside the brown sock so that the white shows through as the head of Jonah and the brown sock as his clothing.

3 Cut bits of black yarn and glue them on for the hair and the beard. Glue on the two wiggle eyes, or use buttons if you prefer.

4 The Jonah puppet goes on your hand and arm. If the socks seem too long just cut the bottoms off to a length that is comfortable for you.

To use your puppet, first put Jonah on your hand, then put your hand in through the back of the fish so that Jonah peeks out of the mouth.

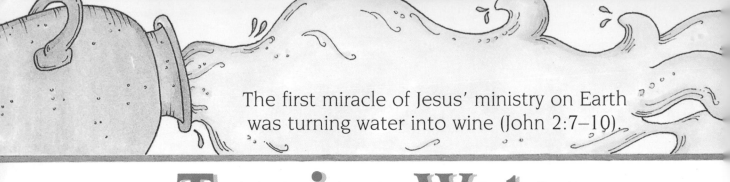

The first miracle of Jesus' ministry on Earth was turning water into wine (John 2:7–10).

Turning Water Into Wine

you need:

ruler

scissors

two uncoated 9-inch (23-cm) paper plates

red, blue, and green markers, crayons, or paints

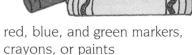

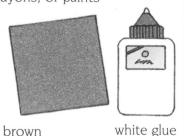

brown construction paper

white glue

paper fastener

what you do:

1 Cut a curved section about 1 1/2 inches (3.75 cm) wide and 6 inches (15 cm) long just below the rim of one of the plates. Color the top (eating side) of the plate green.

2 Hold the cutout plate over the second plate. Use a blue marker to trace around the cutout portion of the first plate on the second plate. Color the traced portion and the area around it blue.

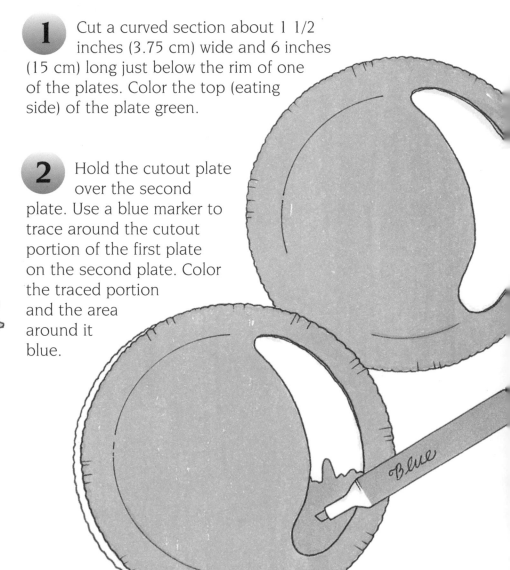

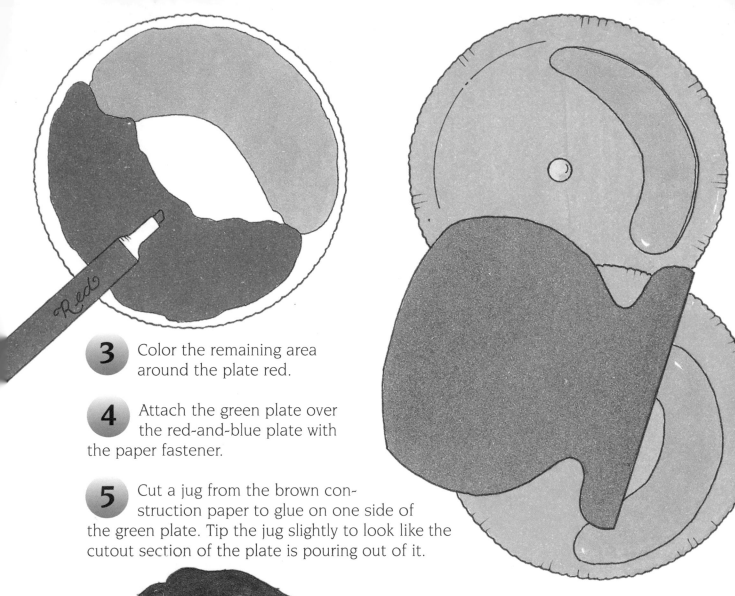

3. Color the remaining area around the plate red.

4. Attach the green plate over the red-and-blue plate with the paper fastener.

5. Cut a jug from the brown construction paper to glue on one side of the green plate. Tip the jug slightly to look like the cutout section of the plate is pouring out of it.

To show Jesus' first miracle start the wheel with the blue showing to represent water flowing from the jug. Slowly turn the back plate to change the blue water to red wine by revealing the red portion of the colored plate.

Stand Up and Walk

you need:

pencil

scissors

ruler

markers

paper fastener

white glue

green, brown, white, and orange construction paper

what you do:

1 Cut a 4- by 10-inch (10- by 25-cm) rectangle from the brown paper for a bed for the crippled man.

2 From the white construction paper, cut the shape of a man with his feet slightly apart. Make him a size that will fit on the bed.

Use markers to give the man a face, hair, and a beard. Cut a garment for the man from the orange paper. Trace around the outside of the figure to get a good fit. Glue the garment on the man.

3 Turn the green paper so that it is longer than it is tall. Lay the bed across the bottom part of the paper. Lay the man on top of the bed. Push the fastener through the right foot, bed, and green paper to attach the bed and the man to the background paper.

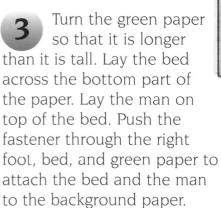

To show what happened when the crippled man trusted in Jesus, stand the man up by swinging the figure on the fastener. Then swing the bed up and tuck it under his arm.

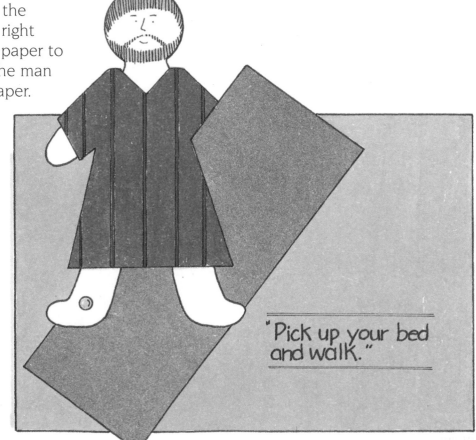

"Pick up your bed and walk."

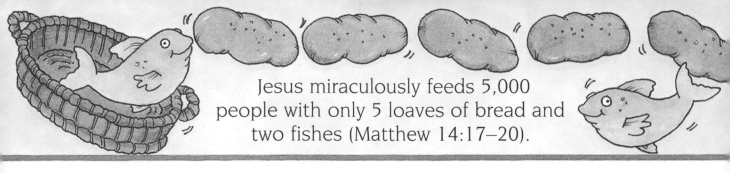

Jesus miraculously feeds 5,000 people with only 5 loaves of bread and two fishes (Matthew 14:17–20).

A Basket With Five Loaves and Two Fishes

you need:

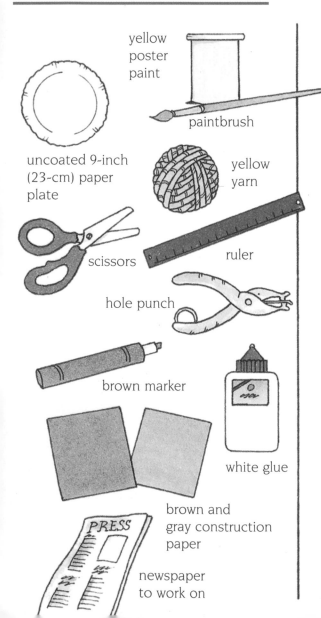

yellow poster paint

paintbrush

uncoated 9-inch (23-cm) paper plate

yellow yarn

scissors

ruler

hole punch

brown marker

white glue

brown and gray construction paper

newspaper to work on

what you do:

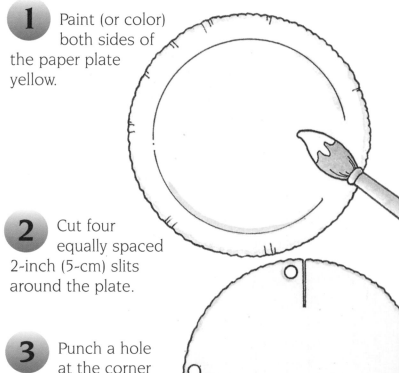

1 Paint (or color) both sides of the paper plate yellow.

2 Cut four equally spaced 2-inch (5-cm) slits around the plate.

3 Punch a hole at the corner of both sides of two sections of the plate that are directly across from each other.

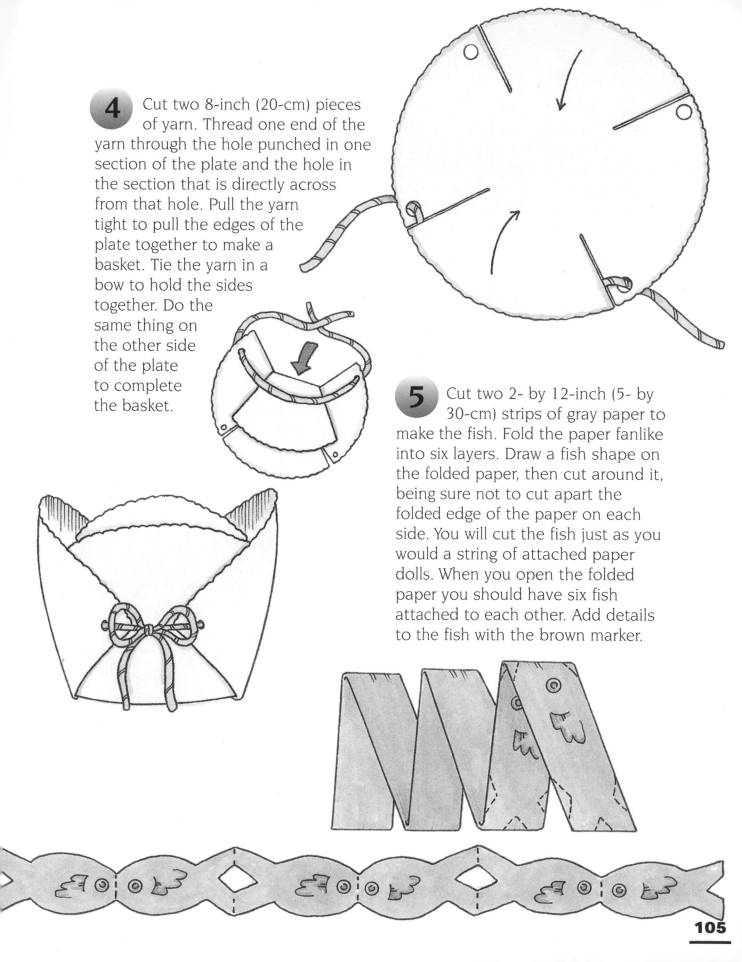

4 Cut two 8-inch (20-cm) pieces of yarn. Thread one end of the yarn through the hole punched in one section of the plate and the hole in the section that is directly across from that hole. Pull the yarn tight to pull the edges of the plate together to make a basket. Tie the yarn in a bow to hold the sides together. Do the same thing on the other side of the plate to complete the basket.

5 Cut two 2- by 12-inch (5- by 30-cm) strips of gray paper to make the fish. Fold the paper fanlike into six layers. Draw a fish shape on the folded paper, then cut around it, being sure not to cut apart the folded edge of the paper on each side. You will cut the fish just as you would a string of attached paper dolls. When you open the folded paper you should have six fish attached to each other. Add details to the fish with the brown marker.

6 To make the loaves of bread cut five 2- by 12-inch (5- by 30-cm) strips of brown paper. Fold the paper fanlike into six layers. Draw the shape of a loaf of bread on the top layer, then cut it out, being sure not to cut apart the folded edge of the paper on each side.

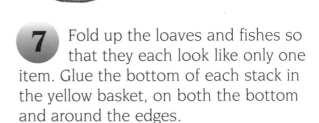

7 Fold up the loaves and fishes so that they each look like only one item. Glue the bottom of each stack in the yellow basket, on both the bottom and around the edges.

To show how Jesus turned five loaves and two fishes into enough to feed 5,000 people, unfold the loaves and fishes to turn a little food into a lot. Sometimes we think we do not have what we need, but Jesus shows us we have more than enough.

Jesus brings a little girl back to life
(Mark 5:41–42).

Jairus's Daughter Puppet

you need:

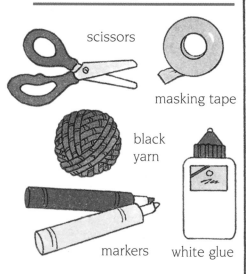

scissors

masking tape

black yarn

markers   white glue

white tube sock

pink construction paper

fabric scrap

salt box with metal pouring spout

shoe-box lid

what you do:

1 Cut the top off the salt box about 1 inch (2.5 cm) below the top.

2 Cover the metal spout with masking tape to create a better gluing surface

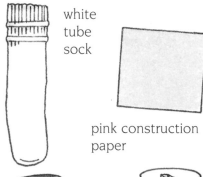

3 Color the top of the box with a marker in skin color for the face of the girl. Draw on facial features with markers, placing the eyes on either side of the spout as shown. Make sure to draw the eyes wide open.

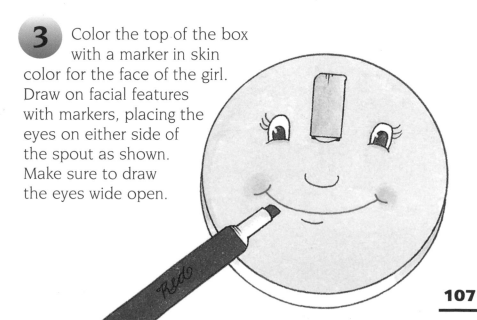

4 Cut two attached eyelids from the pink paper to cover the eyes to make them look closed. Cut several 1-inch (2.5-cm) pieces of yarn and glue them along the bottom of each lid to look like eyelashes. Glue the center of the eyelids to the spout of the salt box. By pushing on the back of the spout you should now be able to open the eyes. Be careful of the back of the metal spout, it might be sharp. Use a piece of fabric to push on it to protect your fingers.

5 Cut bits of yarn for hair and glue them around the head.

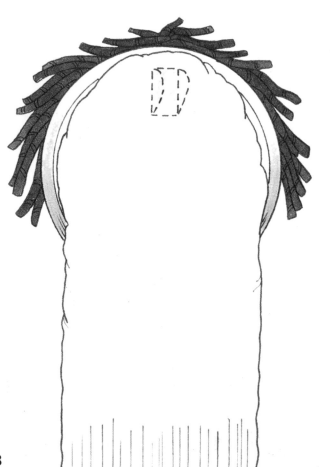

6 Glue the head to the top, toe end of the sock. Be careful not to block your access to the back of the salt spout with too much gluey sock. Cut some sock away if needed.

7 Cut a hole in the center of the shoe-box lid large enough to put your hand through. Put the cuff of the sock down through the hole from the inside of the lid so that the head lies on the box lid like it is a bed. Trim off any excess sock that hangs down below the foot of the box-lid bed when you hold it upright.

8 Cut a square of fabric for a blanket. Put glue only over the inside of the shoe-box lid below the hole, even though the blanket comes up over the hole. Glue the bottom portion of the blanket in the box.

To show what Jesus did for the little girl, put your hand up inside the sock and push the back of the spout to open her eyes. Tip your hand forward to make her sit up and look around. What a wonderful story!

One night Jesus walked across the water to His disciples. But when Peter tried to walk out to meet Him, his faith was overcome by fear and he sank (Matthew 14:28–30).

Jesus Walks on Water

you need:

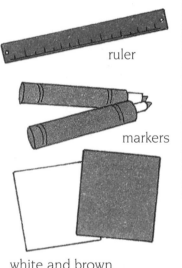

ruler

markers

white and brown construction paper

scissors

white glue

two 9- by 12-inch (23- by 30-cm) sheets of blue construction paper

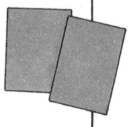

what you do:

1 Draw a 5-inch (13-cm)-tall picture of Jesus and of Peter on the white construction paper to use in your scene. Think about how Jesus might look and feel as He walks across the water full of faith and how Peter would feel as he begins to doubt God and sinks. Cut out the two figures.

2 Cut a shape to represent the front of the boat from the brown construction paper. Make it about 3 inches (8 cm) tall and 5 inches (13 cm) long. Glue the end of the boat to the right side of the paper.

3 Cut a 6-inch (15-cm) slit across the blue paper, starting from the middle of the top of the boat and going toward the center of the paper out of the boat.

4 Glue the cut paper with the boat on it over the second sheet of blue paper, being careful to glue only around the edges of the paper so that you do not glue the slit shut.

5 Glue Jesus in the upper left corner of the paper walking on the water toward the boat. Slip Peter into the boat by sliding him into the slit.

To show what happened, pull Peter up to the top of the slit to move him out of the boat and onto the water. After he is on the water, slide him down into the slit in the paper to make it look like he is sinking in the water.

Jesus wants us to trust in Him.

Ten men are healed by Jesus, but only one man came back to tell Jesus he was grateful (Luke 17:15–18).

A Story About Gratitude

you need:

12- by 18-inch (30- by 46-cm) sheet of white construction paper

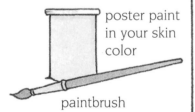

poster paint in your skin color

paintbrush

markers

newspaper to work on

what you do:

1 Fold the white sheet of paper in half so that you have a 9- by 12-inch (23- by 30-cm) card that opens from the top.

2 Paint your hands, one at a time, and print them on the front of the paper.

3 Open the paper up carefully so you do not smear the handprints (or wait until they are dry) and print your two fists inside the paper. To do this, close the fingers of your hand and paint over the palm and knuckles, then press the closed hand on the paper. You will need to roll the closed hand back and forth a bit to paint the entire area to look like a fist.

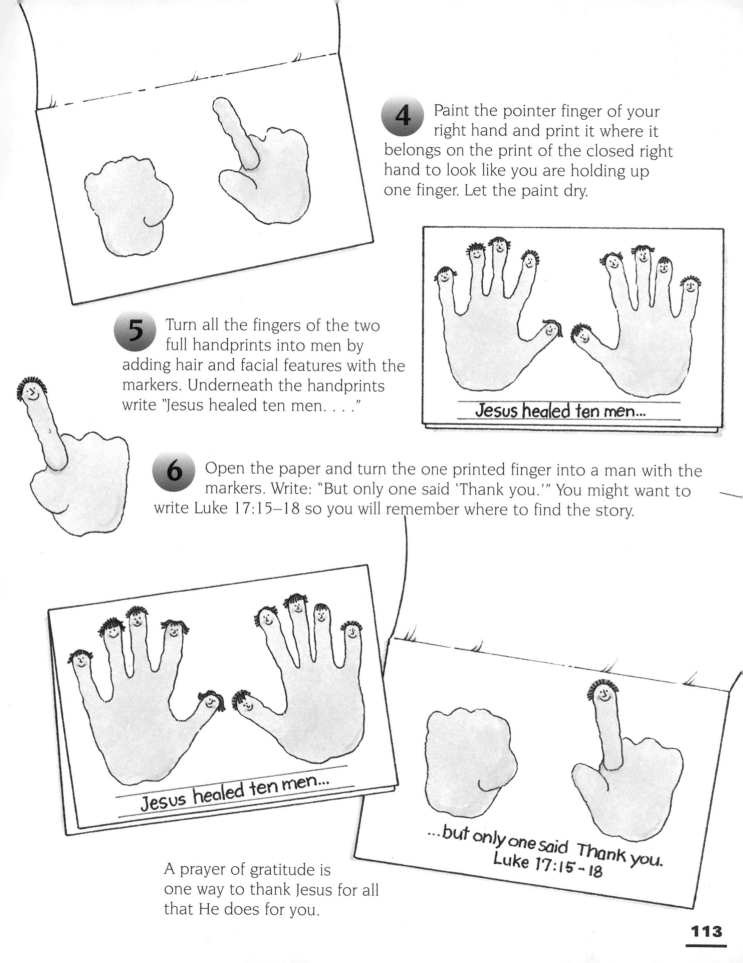

4 Paint the pointer finger of your right hand and print it where it belongs on the print of the closed right hand to look like you are holding up one finger. Let the paint dry.

5 Turn all the fingers of the two full handprints into men by adding hair and facial features with the markers. Underneath the handprints write "Jesus healed ten men. . . ."

Jesus healed ten men...

6 Open the paper and turn the one printed finger into a man with the markers. Write: "But only one said 'Thank you.'" You might want to write Luke 17:15–18 so you will remember where to find the story.

Jesus healed ten men...

...but only one said Thank you.
Luke 17:15 - 18

A prayer of gratitude is one way to thank Jesus for all that He does for you.

The people of Jerusalem welcomed Jesus with palm branches (Matthew 21:8–9).

Waving Palms

you need:

scissors

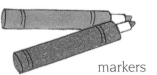

markers

two uncoated 9-inch (23-cm) paper plates

paper fastener

what you do:

1 Cut a half-circle piece out of the inner rim of one plate that does not quite go all the way to the middle of the plate.

2 Use the markers to draw a person below the cut opening of the plate. The hands of the person should reach up to the opening. Also color in the background around the person.

3 Use the paper fastener to attach the center of the cut plate over the center of the second plate.

4 Draw a curved palm on the exposed area of the bottom plate in each hand of the person.

5 Carefully turn the back plate in one direction and extend the drawing of the palms on the exposed portion of the back plate. Turn the plate in the other direction and do the same thing. Color the area around the palms blue for sky.

6 Write: "Hosanna! Blessed is He who comes in the name of the Lord" above the palms.

Blue

Turn the back plate back and forth to show the person waving palms in celebration of Jesus' arrival.

Hosanna! Blessed is he who comes in the name of the LORD!

Matthew 21 Luke 19

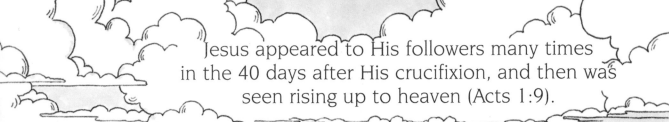

Jesus appeared to His followers many times in the 40 days after His crucifixion, and then was seen rising up to heaven (Acts 1:9).

Jesus Ascends

you need:

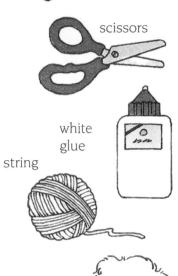

markers

scissors

white glue

string

fiberfill

sliding matchbox

what you do:

1 Slide the inner box out of the matchbox. Use the markers to draw a picture of Jesus on the bottom of the box.

2 Poke a small hole through the side of the box above the head of the drawing.

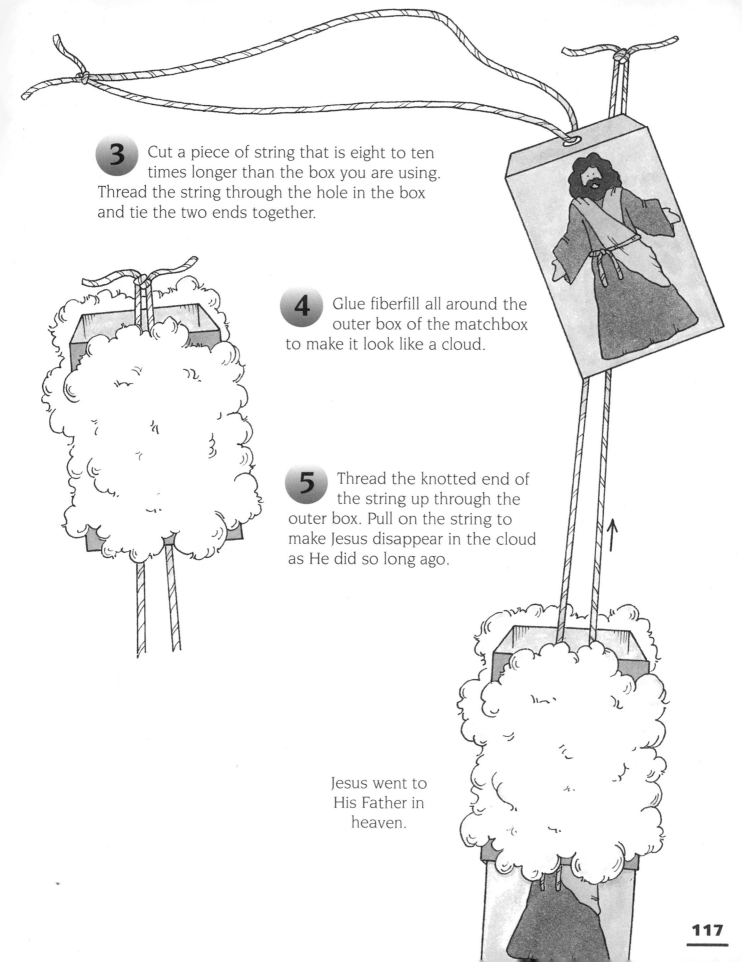

3 Cut a piece of string that is eight to ten times longer than the box you are using. Thread the string through the hole in the box and tie the two ends together.

4 Glue fiberfill all around the outer box of the matchbox to make it look like a cloud.

5 Thread the knotted end of the string up through the outer box. Pull on the string to make Jesus disappear in the cloud as He did so long ago.

Jesus went to His Father in heaven.

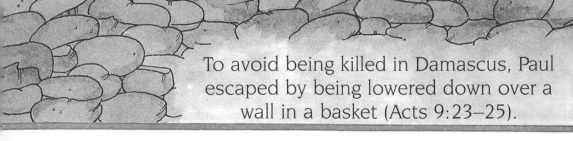

To avoid being killed in Damascus, Paul escaped by being lowered down over a wall in a basket (Acts 9:23–25).

Paul Over the Wall

you need:

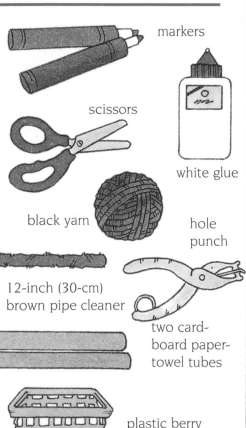

markers

white glue

scissors

black yarn

hole punch

12-inch (30-cm) brown pipe cleaner

two cardboard paper-towel tubes

plastic berry basket

large cork

9- by 12-inch (23- by 30-cm) piece of lightweight cardboard

what you do:

1 Use a marker to draw the outline of stones all over one side of the cardboard to make it look like a wall.

2 Glue a cardboard tube on the back of each side of the wall to make the wall stand up.

3 To make the basket in which Paul can escape, cut two sides from the berry basket, leaving them attached at the corner. Fold the two sides in together and weave the brown pipe cleaner in and out to close the bottom and open side. Trim off any extra pipe cleaner.

4 Cut two pieces of yarn, each twice as long as the height of the wall. Punch two holes in the top of the wall the same distance apart as the width of the basket. Thread one of the pieces of yarn through one side of the basket. Thread both ends of the yarn through the hole at the top of the wall directly above that side of the basket. Do the same thing with the second piece of yarn on the other side of the basket. Tie the four ends of yarn together behind the wall. You should now be able to move the basket up and down the wall by pulling and releasing the knotted ends of yarn behind the wall.

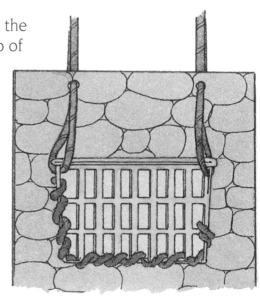

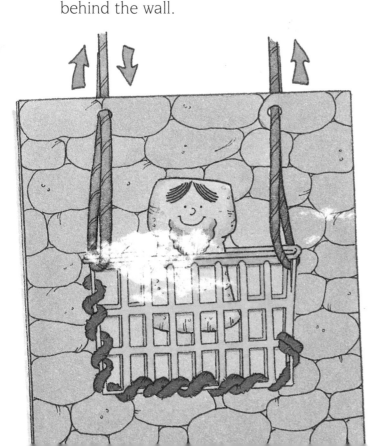

5 Use markers to color the cork to look like Paul. Put the cork into the basket.

Quick! Help Paul escape from Damascus by lowering him down over the wall in the basket!

Christian Values

Remember to be thankful for all that you have been given.
"THANKFUL FOR MY FOOD" BOOK 138

Attend church every week to worship and learn about God.
CHURCH ATTENDANCE STABILE 141

Remember to use good manners.
GOOD MANNERS PUPPET 142

To have empathy is to try to understand how
someone else might feel.
CHEERFUL COOKIE BOX 144

Recycling is a way of caring for the world that God has given us.
RECYCLED CRAYONS 146

Be forgiving of others.
FORGIVENESS BRACELET 148

Being tolerant means trying to understand and accept
people who are different from you.
GOD'S WORLD BOOK 150

Cooperation means working together for the good of the group.
COOPERATION TULIPS 152

Keep a loving heart.

Loving Heart Beanbag

you need:

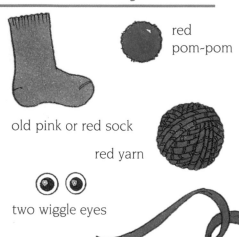

old pink or red sock

red yarn

red pom-pom

two wiggle eyes

thin red ribbon

scissors

stapler

white glue

pencil

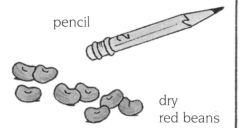
dry red beans

what you do:

1 Cut off the foot of the sock about 5 inches (13 cm) from the toe end. Trim the cut end to form two bumps to look like the top of a heart.

2 Turn the sock inside out. Starting at the center of the toe, staple the two sides of the sock into a point to form the bottom of the heart. Turn the sock right-side out.

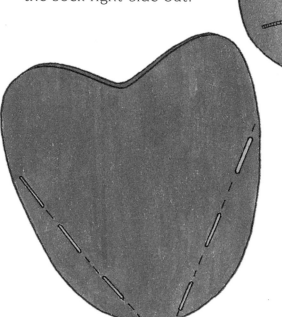

122

3 Glue the front and back of the heart together, leaving an opening between the two bumps just large enough to slip a bean through.

4 Cut a 10-inch (25-cm) length of red ribbon. Use the pencil to push one end of the ribbon through the front and back of the sock weave at the opening at the top of the heart. Tie the ribbon in a bow to close the opening.

5

Cut a 1-inch (2.5-cm) piece of red yarn. Glue it on the front of the heart for a smile. Glue on the two wiggle eyes and the red pom-pom nose to complete the face.

Whenever you do something kind for someone, untie the ribbon and put a bean in your beanbag heart, then tie it closed again. How long will it take you to fill your heart? What a nice way to remember to keep a loving heart!

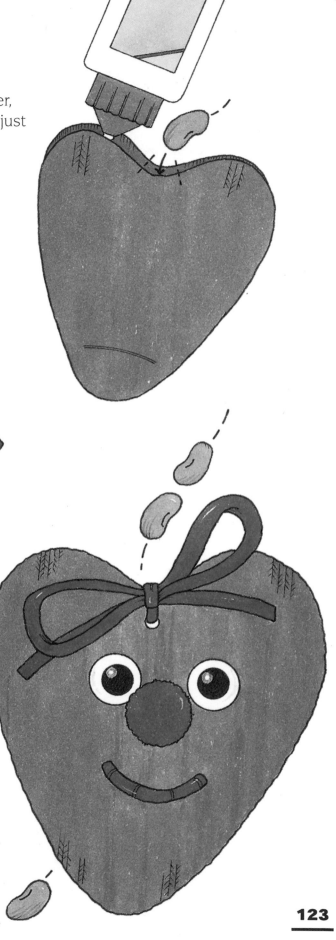

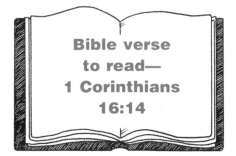

Bible verse to read— 1 Corinthians 16:14

Lamb Mission Bank

you need:

black knit glove

fiberfill

thin red ribbon

white paper scrap

black marker

scissors

hole punch

Styrofoam tray to work on

white glue

stapler

what you do:

1 Cut a 1-foot (30-cm) length of red ribbon. Staple one end to the inside of each side of the opening of the glove to make a hanger.

2 Cover the palm and half the thumb of the glove with glue, then cover the glue with fiberfill. Turn the glove over and do the same thing on the other side.

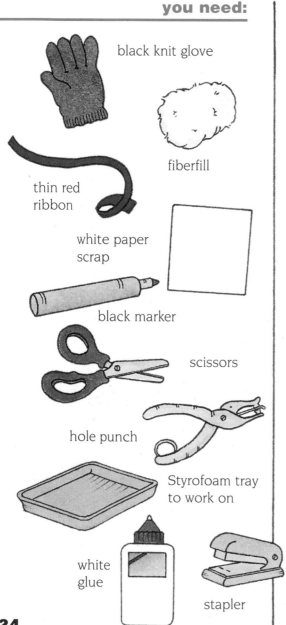

This will be the body of the sheep with the four fingers hanging down for the legs and the thumb forming the head.

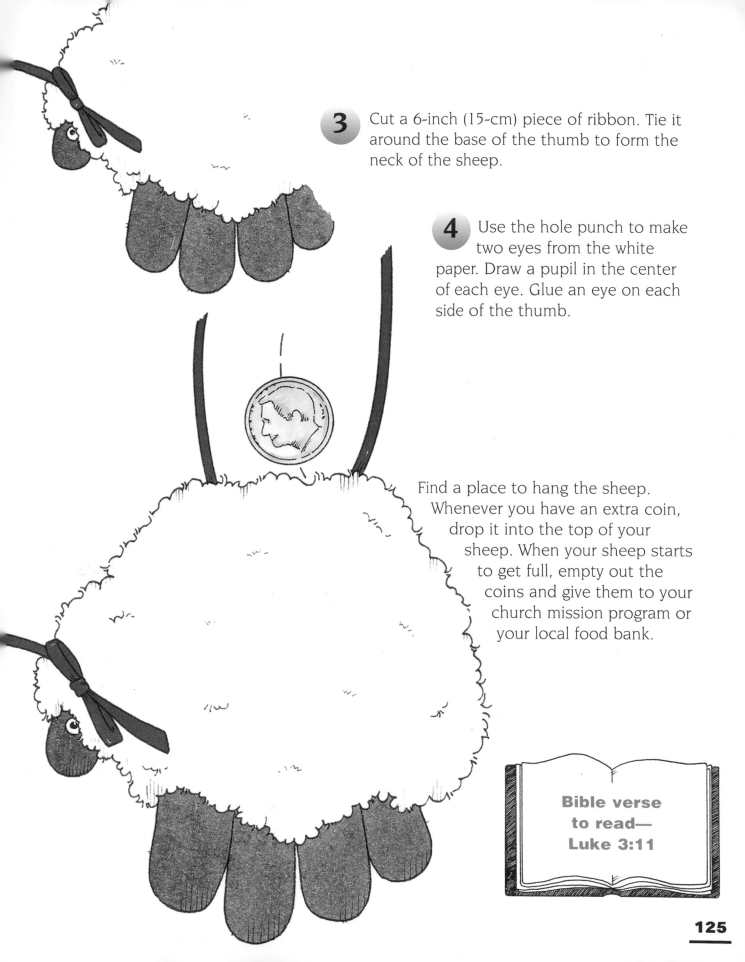

3 Cut a 6-inch (15-cm) piece of ribbon. Tie it around the base of the thumb to form the neck of the sheep.

4 Use the hole punch to make two eyes from the white paper. Draw a pupil in the center of each eye. Glue an eye on each side of the thumb.

Find a place to hang the sheep. Whenever you have an extra coin, drop it into the top of your sheep. When your sheep starts to get full, empty out the coins and give them to your church mission program or your local food bank.

Bible verse to read— Luke 3:11

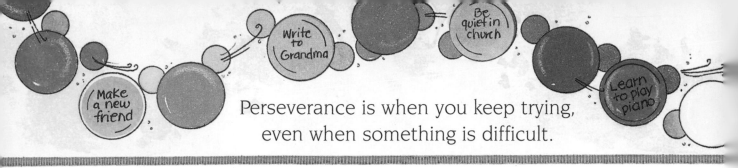

Accomplishment Pencil Can

you need:

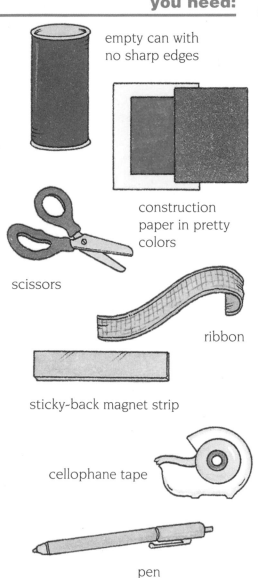

empty can with no sharp edges

construction paper in pretty colors

scissors

ribbon

sticky-back magnet strip

cellophane tape

pen

what you do:

1 Cut a strip of construction paper to fit around the can to cover it. Tape the paper in place around the can.

2 Tie a pretty ribbon around the top of the can.

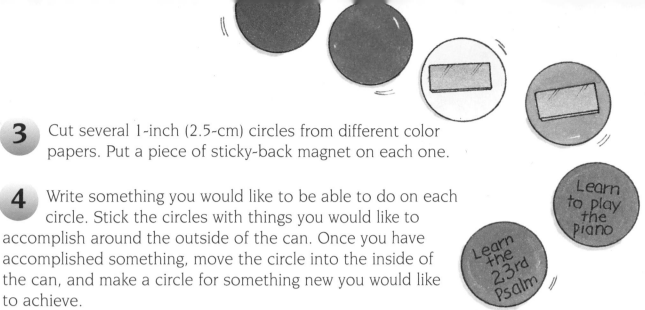

3 Cut several 1-inch (2.5-cm) circles from different color papers. Put a piece of sticky-back magnet on each one.

4 Write something you would like to be able to do on each circle. Stick the circles with things you would like to accomplish around the outside of the can. Once you have accomplished something, move the circle into the inside of the can, and make a circle for something new you would like to achieve.

Keep the accomplishment can on your desk for your pencils and pens. It will serve as a reminder to work hard at being the person that God wants you to be.

Bible verse
to read—
Galatians 6:9

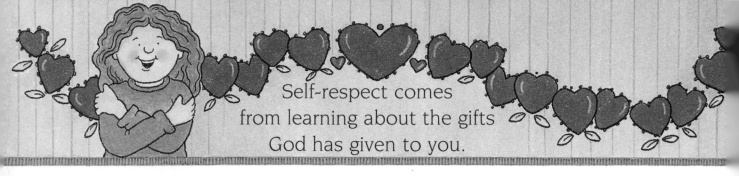

Self-respect comes
from learning about the gifts
God has given to you.

Thoughts Box

you need:

sturdy cardboard box

photo or drawing of you

white glue

markers

pen

pad of sticky notes

what you do:

1 Decorate the lid of the box by gluing a picture of you in the center. Use the markers to write, "I look this way outside of me." You can also add whatever other words and drawings you would like to decorate the lid.

I look this way outside of me.

2 On the inside of the box keep a pen and a pad of sticky notes. Use them to write down your thoughts and feelings, then stick them in the box. You might want to add the date, too.

You will quickly have to layer the thoughts one on top of the other with so many thoughts and feelings going through your head every day. Go through the notes after a few weeks. Did God change your mind about the way you feel about something? Were you concerned about something that turned out fine? Do you wish you felt differently about something? Use your "thoughts box" to draw nearer to God.

Bible verse to read— Proverbs 19:8

Bottle-Cap Photo Frames

you need:

one or two plastic flip-top lids at least 1½ inches (3.75 cm) across

photo or drawing of each of your parents

pen

masking tape

trim

white glue

scissors

what you do:

1 Find or make a small picture of your parent to put in the bottle-cap frame. Center the lid over the face in the photo and trace around the lid with the pen. Cut the picture out.

2 Cut a piece of pretty trim long enough to fit around the outside of the lid.

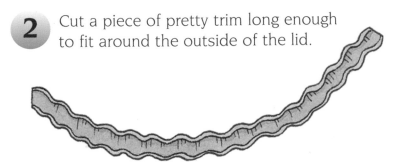

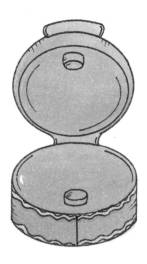

Open the flip-top. Glue the trim around the outside of the lid, overlapping the ends of the trim opposite the flip-top hinge.

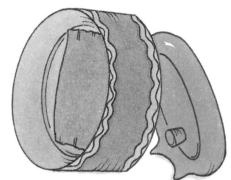

3 Put a piece of masking tape inside the top to create a better gluing surface. Stand your frame up by using the opened top like an easel to prop up the cap picture frame. If you glued a picture of your Mom in the frame, make a second one for your Dad.

Put the little pictures of your Mom and Dad in a place where you can see them often and be reminded of how important they are to you.

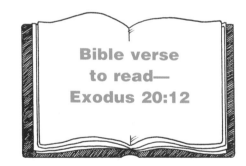

Bible verse to read—
Exodus 20:12

Love your family.

My Family Bookmark

you need:

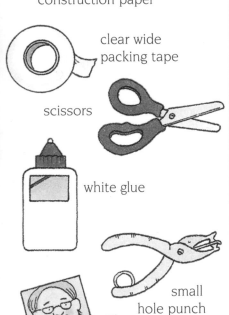

construction paper

clear wide
packing tape

scissors

white glue

small
hole punch

photographs
of the people
in your family

thin ribbon
in two colors

what you do:

1 From the photographs, cut out just the heads of each of your family members. If you have a very small family, use more than one photo of each person. If you do not have any photos for this craft, draw pictures of the head of each family member.

2 Glue the heads on the construction paper to form a long strip. Let the glue dry before continuing.

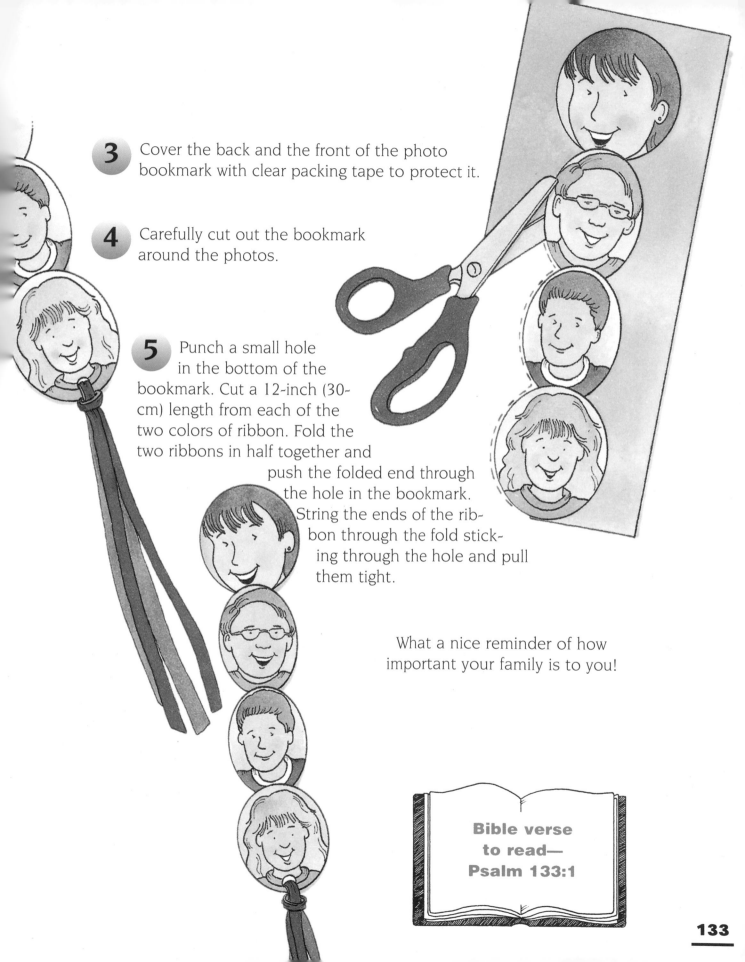

3 Cover the back and the front of the photo bookmark with clear packing tape to protect it.

4 Carefully cut out the bookmark around the photos.

5 Punch a small hole in the bottom of the bookmark. Cut a 12-inch (30-cm) length from each of the two colors of ribbon. Fold the two ribbons in half together and push the folded end through the hole in the bookmark. String the ends of the ribbon through the fold sticking through the hole and pull them tight.

What a nice reminder of how important your family is to you!

Bible verse to read— Psalm 133:1

Be helpful.

Helpful Hand Magnet

you need:

access to a copy machine

white copy paper

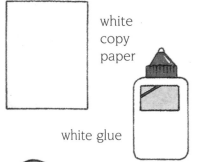

white glue

scissors

clear wide packing tape

colorful macaroni craft letters

sticky-back magnet

what you do:

1 Ask an adult to help you copy your hand on a copy machine, then reduce the height of the hand to about 2 inches (5 cm).

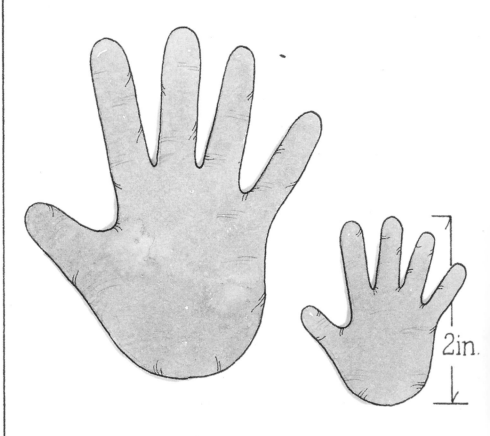

2in.

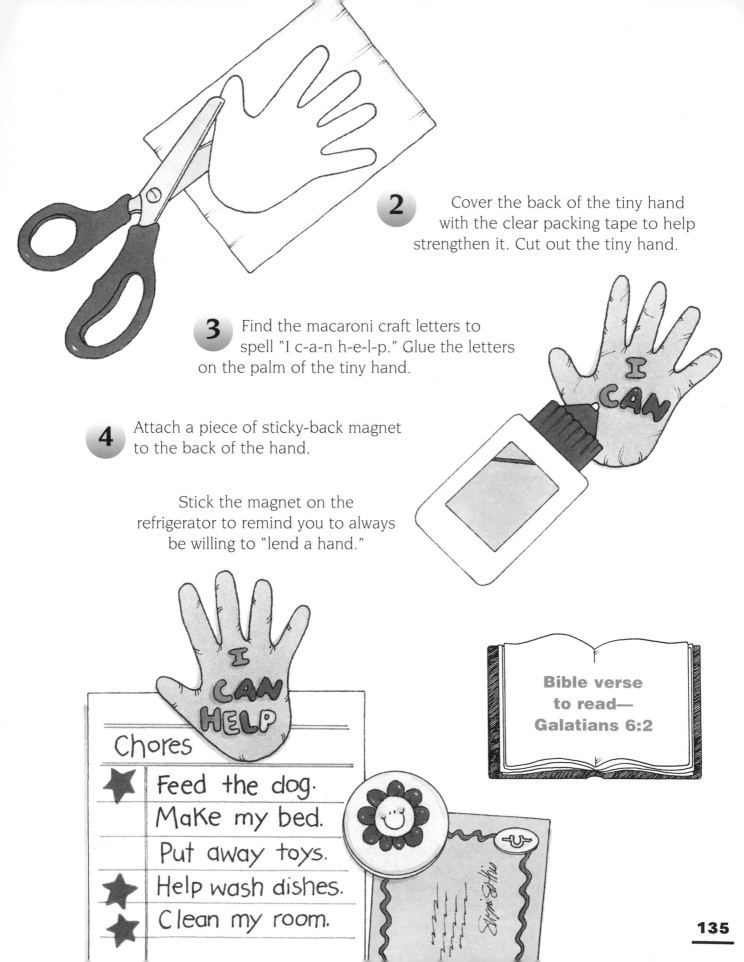

2 Cover the back of the tiny hand with the clear packing tape to help strengthen it. Cut out the tiny hand.

3 Find the macaroni craft letters to spell "I c-a-n h-e-l-p." Glue the letters on the palm of the tiny hand.

4 Attach a piece of sticky-back magnet to the back of the hand.

Stick the magnet on the refrigerator to remind you to always be willing to "lend a hand."

I CAN HELP

Chores
★ Feed the dog.
Make my bed.
Put away toys.
★ Help wash dishes.
★ Clean my room.

Bible verse
to read—
Galatians 6:2

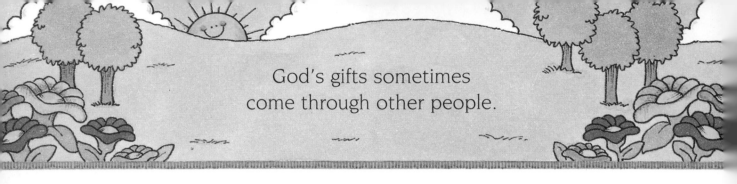

God's gifts sometimes
come through other people.

Gratitude Jar

you need:

large plastic
jar with a
screw-on lid

two buttons

red pipe cleaner

old colored sock

thin ribbon

red construction
paper

pen

scissors

cellophane tape

paper and pencil

what you do:

1 Soak the jar in warm water to remove the label and glue.

2 Cut a 3-inch (8-cm) heart from the red construction paper. Write "Thank you God for the kindness of others" on the front of the heart. Tape the heart inside the jar so that you can read the words through the plastic jar.

3 Tape the two buttons to the inside top of the jar above the heart to look like eyes.

4 Cut a 1-inch (2.5-cm) piece of pipe cleaner and shape it into a smile. Tape the smile inside the jar just below the eyes.

5 Cut about 4 inches (10 cm) off the cuff of the sock to use for a hat. Cut an 8-inch (20-cm) length of ribbon and tie it around the cut end of the cuff piece to close it. Tie the ribbon in a pretty bow. Put the cuff over the lid of the jar to look like a hat.

6 Keep notepaper and the pencil beside the jar, so you can write down the kind things that others have done for you. Store the notes in your gratitude jar.

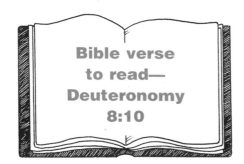

God works through His people. The "gratitude jar" will help you remember the many kindnesses you have received from other people. Maybe you will want to help fill the "gratitude jars" of others!

Bible verse to read— Deuteronomy 8:10

Remember
to be thankful for all
that you have been given.

"Thankful for My Food" Book

you need:

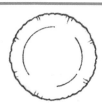

14 uncoated
white paper
plates

hole punch

yarn

scissors

cellophane
tape

markers

what you do:

1 Stack two plates on top of each other and punch a series of holes through the rims of both, spaced about 1 1/2 to 2 inches (4 to 5 cm) apart.

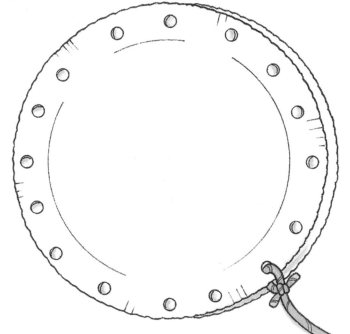

2 Cut a 2-foot (60-cm) length of yarn for each plate. Tie one end of the yarn through a hole in one of the plates. Wrap the other end of the yarn with cellophane tape to make a "needle" to sew with.

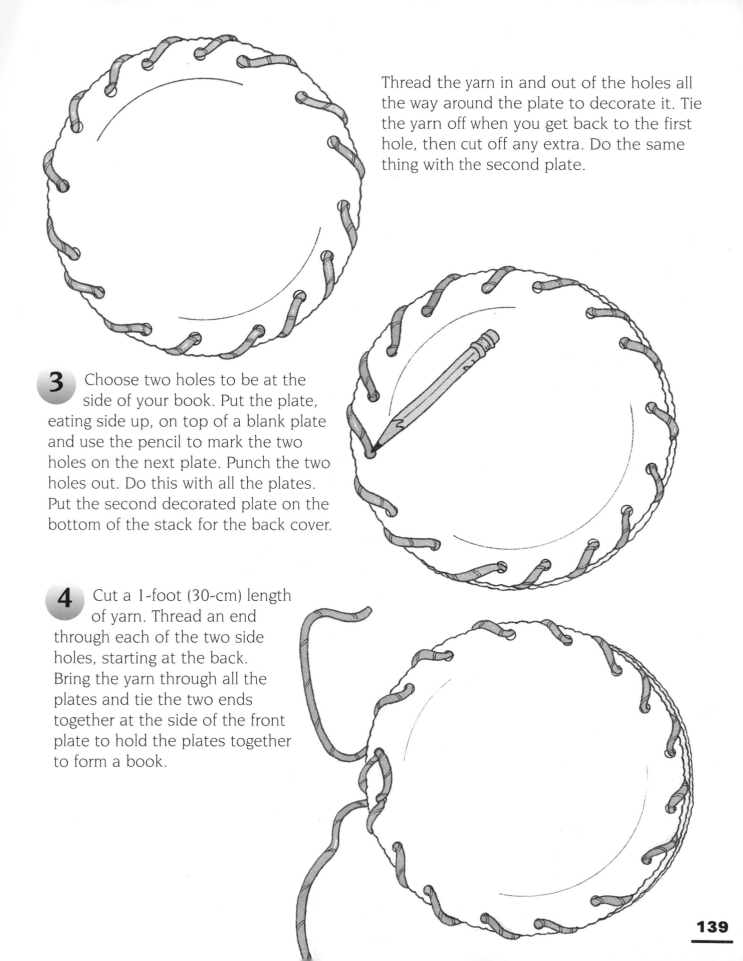

Thread the yarn in and out of the holes all the way around the plate to decorate it. Tie the yarn off when you get back to the first hole, then cut off any extra. Do the same thing with the second plate.

3 Choose two holes to be at the side of your book. Put the plate, eating side up, on top of a blank plate and use the pencil to mark the two holes on the next plate. Punch the two holes out. Do this with all the plates. Put the second decorated plate on the bottom of the stack for the back cover.

4 Cut a 1-foot (30-cm) length of yarn. Thread an end through each of the two side holes, starting at the back. Bring the yarn through all the plates and tie the two ends together at the side of the front plate to hold the plates together to form a book.

My Prayer

5 Use the markers to decorate the front of the book. You might want to write your favorite mealtime prayer on the cover. On each plate inside draw a picture of one of your favorite foods.

Thank you for Pizza!

and pepperoni!

My Prayer

Thank you for the world so sweet.
Thank you for the food we eat.
Thank you for the birds that sing.
Thank you God, for everything.
Amen.

Remember to give thanks to God for your food.

Bible verse to read— Ephesians 5:18, 20

140

Attend church every week to worship and learn about God.

Church Attendance Stabile

you need:

clay or Play-Doh™

pipe cleaners

variety of beads, buttons, and jingle bells

what you do:

1 Roll a 2-inch (5-cm) ball of clay or Play-Doh™ for the base of the stabile.

2 Cut three pieces of pipe cleaner 4 to 6 inches (10 to 15 cm) long. Stick the ends of the pipe cleaners into the top of the Play-Doh™ ball.

3 Each week that you attend church, choose a bead, button, or bell to string on one of the pipe cleaners.

Add something each week until the stems of the stabile are filled. You might want to keep your stabile at church until it is finished.

Bible verse to read— Psalm 122:1

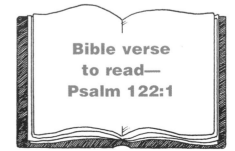

141

Good Manners Puppet

you need:

skin-tone and red construction paper

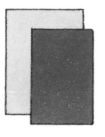

stapler

small pudding box

yarn bits

white glue

masking tape

marker

scissors

what you do:

1 Tape the open end of the box closed. Cut around the front and two sides of the box at the center. Fold the box in half over the uncut side. The box will form a face with the fold being the mouth.

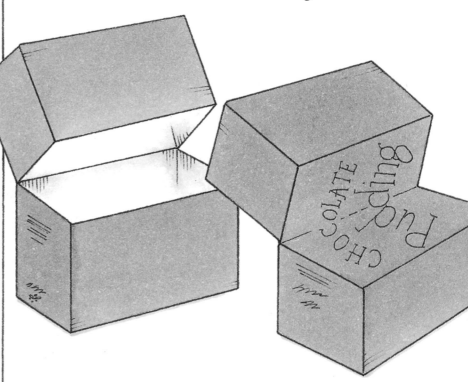

2 Flatten the box and trace around the front on the red paper. Cut the traced shape out. You will need six of this shape to make a little book.

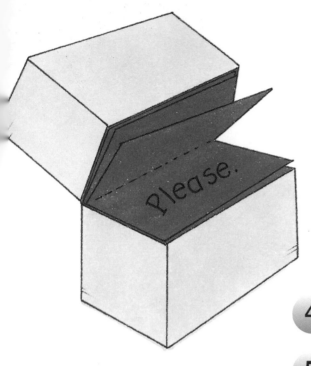

3 Stack the six red sheets together and fold them in half to fit inside the folded mouth of the puppet. Staple the papers at the fold to hold them together. Write something polite that a person might say on each page of the book. Glue the book inside the puppet's mouth.

4 Cover the top and bottom parts of the puppet's face with the skin-tone construction paper.

5 Glue yarn bits to the top of the puppet for hair.

6 Use the marker to give the puppet eyes and a nose above the mouth.

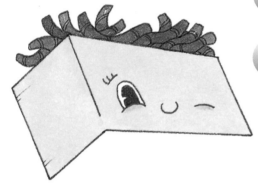

This is a very polite puppet!

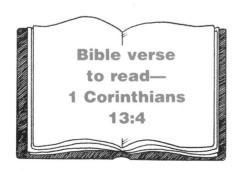

Bible verse
to read—
1 Corinthians
13:4

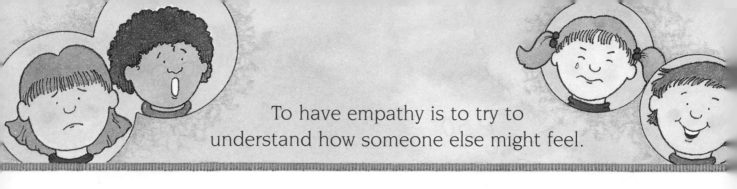

To have empathy is to try to understand how someone else might feel.

Cheerful Cookie Box

you need:

two identical disposable plastic containers with lids

photos, drawings, and old greeting cards

scissors

sticky bow

what you do:

1 Cut a total of four different pictures to fit, with the edges slightly overlapping, around the four sides of one of the containers.

2 Lightly set one container inside the other. Slide the pictures down between the two containers to cover the four sides. Press the inner container down to secure the pictures in place between them.

3 Place a lid on the top container. Stick a sticky bow on the center of the lid.

Fill the container with some yummy cookies and surprise someone who might be feeling sad or lonely.

Bible verse to read— 1 Corinthians 9:22

Recycling is a way of caring for the world
that God has given us.

Recycled Crayons

you need:

foil cupcake wrappers

old crayon stubs

zip-to-close
plastic bag

wooden mallet

what you do:

1 Peel the wrappers off several old crayons of similar shades of color.

2 Put the pieces in a zip-to-close plastic bag and seal it, first squeezing out as much air as possible. Gently tap on the crayons with the mallet to break them into smaller pieces. The smaller the crayon bits, the faster they will melt together.

3

Fill a foil muffin cup with crayon pieces about three-quarters full.

4

Put the cup in the hot sun to melt the crayon bits into a big new crayon. If it is too cold to melt the crayons, ask an adult to place the cup in a 250-degree oven on a foil-covered cookie sheet for a few minutes until the crayons melt together.

5 Let the crayon cup air-cool, then pop it out of the foil wrapper.

Use old crayons to make lots of new crayons in different shades and colors.

Bible verse to read— Psalm 33:5

Be forgiving of others.

Forgiveness Bracelet

you need:

clear plastic
16-ounce
soda bottle

trim

sharp marker

construction
paper

scissors

yarn

small
hole punch

white glue

what you do:

1 If the bottle has a paper label on it, remove it. Ask an adult to cut off the top part of the bottle — the part where it slants in. Cut down the side of the remaining part of the bottle to the bottom. Cut two identical rings from the bottle, each about 1/2 inch (1.25 cm) wide.

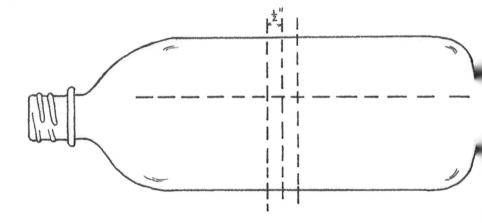

2 Cut a strip of construction paper the same size as the two rings.

Forgive and you will be forgiven. – Luke 6.37

3 Write a Bible verse about forgiveness on the paper, such as "Forgive and you will be forgiven" from the Book of Luke. Decorate the strip by gluing trim across the top and the bottom. Let the glue dry.

Forgive and you will be forgiven-Luke 6.37

4 Put the two plastic strips together with the paper strip in between them. Punch a hole at each end through all three layers.

5 Cut a 6-inch (15-cm) piece of yarn. Thread an end through each hole in the bracelet and tie the ends together, making the bracelet as large or small as you need it to be to slip it on over your hand.

Wear this bracelet as a reminder to forgive others as God forgives you.

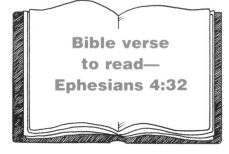

Bible verse to read— Ephesians 4:32

Being tolerant means trying to understand and accept people who are different from you.

God's World Book

you need:

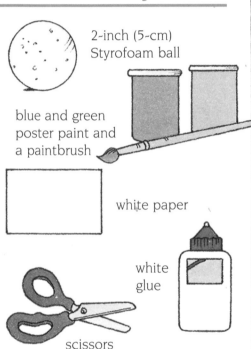

2-inch (5-cm) Styrofoam ball

blue and green poster paint and a paintbrush

white paper

white glue

scissors

thin ribbon

pictures from old magazines and catalogs of people from around the world

Styrofoam tray to work on

what you do:

1 Ask an adult to cut the Styrofoam ball in half. Paint the outside of both halves blue to look like the water on the Earth. Dab some green paint over the blue on each half to look like landforms. Let the two halves dry on the Styrofoam tray.

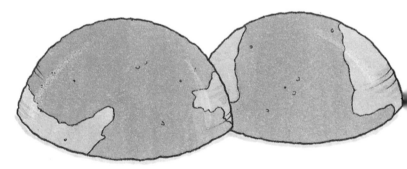

2 Trace around the flat end of one of the balls on the edge of the white paper.

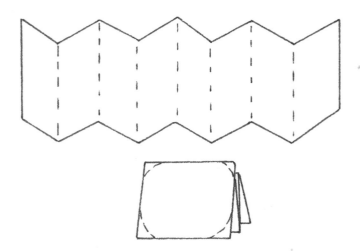

Fold the paper back and forth to make an accordion book the width of the circle. Cut around the top and bottom of the traced circle to make the accordion book fit between the two halves of the Styrofoam ball Earth.

3 Glue the back of the front page to the left side of the Earth and the last page to the right side of the Earth so that the two halves become the front and back cover of the accordion book.

4 Find pictures of God's people from around the world. Glue a different picture on each page of the book.

5 Close the book by tying the two halves of the Earth together with a ribbon.

Learn more about people who look or live in a way different from you.

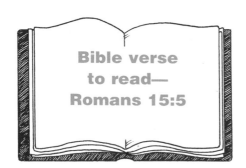

Bible verse
to read—
Romans 15:5

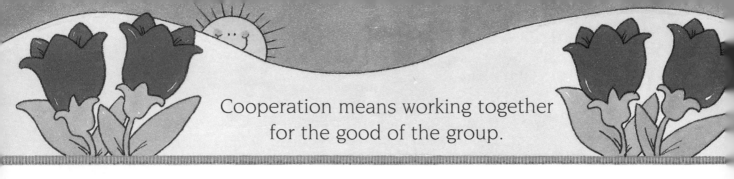

Cooperation means working together
for the good of the group.

Cooperation Tulips

what you do:

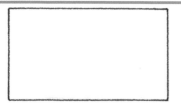

four large sheets of
white construction paper

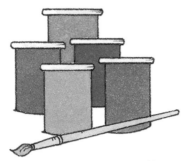

poster paint in green and
four pretty colors and five
paintbrushes

 marker

three friends to work with you

newspaper to
work on

1 Each person should write his or her own
name on the top of one paper.

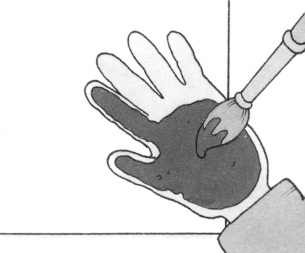

Michael

2 Each person should choose one color,
besides green, to use. Each person needs to use
a different color. The first person paints a hand with the
chosen color, then, with fingers and thumb together,
prints a hand tulip on the top left of each of the four
papers. The hand may need to be repainted for each
paper to get a good print.

3 The next person does the same thing, printing a hand tulip in the space next to the first one. Continue until each person has printed a tulip on each of the four papers. Everyone will need to wash their hands before continuing.

4 Each person may now go to his or her own paper and use the green paint to give each tulip a stem and some leaves.

5 Use the marker to write the name of the friend under the tulip that he or she printed.

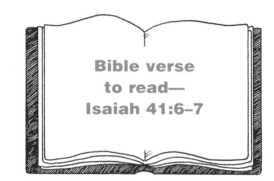

Bible verse
to read—
Isaiah 41:6–7

Cooperating is such fun!

Michael

Michael   kevin   Dave   Pat

153

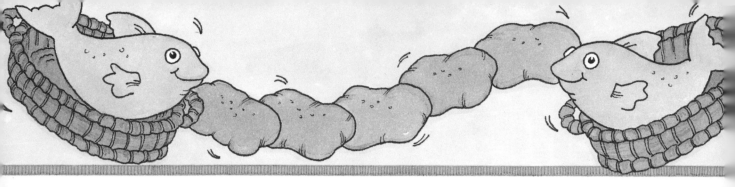

Christian Witness

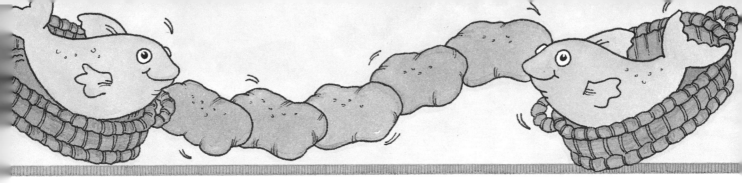

Be filled with joy!

Joyful Noise Hat

you need:

old cardboard party hat

old party blower

light-color construction paper

markers

scissors

white glue

masking tape

stickers

what you do:

1 Carefully unglue the seam of the hat and flatten it to use as a pattern. Use a marker to trace around the hat on the construction paper. Cut the hat shape out.

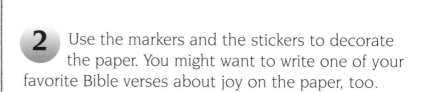

2 Use the markers and the stickers to decorate the paper. You might want to write one of your favorite Bible verses about joy on the paper, too.

Make a Joyful Noise to the Lord all the Earth.

3 Glue the paper over the cardboard hat. Glue the seam of the hat back together.

4 Cut the cardboard part off the party blower so that you only have the plastic blower from the end.

5 Cut just enough off the point of the hat so that the cut end of the blower will fit down through the hole. Use the masking tape to hold the blower in place inside the hat. The end you blow into should stick out from the top of the hat.

When you wear your "joyful" hat you will be ready to make a joyful noise by taking the hat off and blowing on the horn.

Bible verse to read Psalm 100: 1–2

God tells us to share what
we have with others.

Loaves and Fishes Pin

you need:

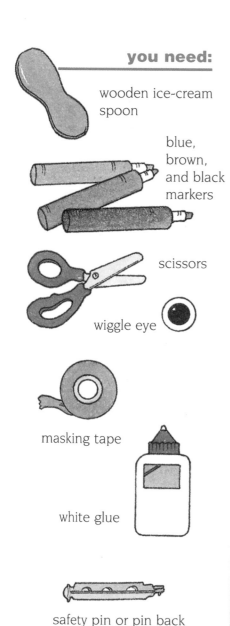

wooden ice-cream
spoon

blue,
brown,
and black
markers

scissors

wiggle eye

masking tape

white glue

safety pin or pin back

what you do:

1 Cut the spoon in half. The larger end of
the spoon will be the fish. Trim the cut
end to look like the tail of a fish. The smaller
half of the spoon will be the loaf of bread.
Round off the corners of the cut end.

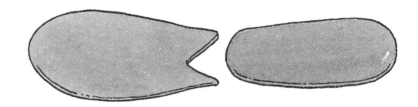

2 Color the fish blue. Use the black marker
to add detail such as scales and fins.

3 Put a piece of masking tape on the back of the wiggle eye to create a better gluing surface. Glue the wiggle eye to the head of the fish.

4 Color the loaf of bread with the brown marker.

5 Glue the fish to one side of the loaf of bread so that the bread is still visible.

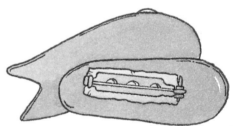

6 Put a piece of masking tape on the side of the safety pin or pin back that will be glued to the back of the loaf of bread to create a better gluing surface. Glue on the pin back or safety pin and let the glue dry.

Wear this pin as a reminder of the wonderful miracle that Jesus performed with what one little boy was willing to share (Matthew 14:17–20).

Bible verse to read— Hebrews 13:16

Cross Pin

you need:

eight small gold
safety pins

seed beads in
two colors (make
sure the openings
are large enough
to string on
safety pins)

what you do:

1 Open one safety pin and put on seed beads of one color, then close the safety pin to hold them in place. It will take about eight beads. Because pins can vary, the number of beads needed might vary too, but the idea will still work. Do the same thing with the second safety pin.

2 On the next four safety pins put on four beads of the same color as the first two safety pins, then one bead of the second color, then three more beads of the first color. Close each safety pin to hold the beads in place.

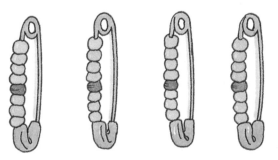

3 On the next safety pin put all beads of the second color, then close the safety pin.

4 Open the last safety pin. You are going to thread each safety pin onto the open part of the pin under the head of each closed pin, then slide them around to the back bar of the pin. You need to end up with the beads facing outward when hanging down from the back bar of the holder safety pin. The beaded safety pins must be put on in the following order: 1. safety pin with all first-color beads; 2. and 3. safety pins with seven first-color beads and one second-color bead; 4. safety pin with all second-color beads; 5. and 6. safety pin with seven first-color and one second-color beads; 7. safety pin with all first-color beads. When all the beaded safety pins hang down together, they should form a cross.

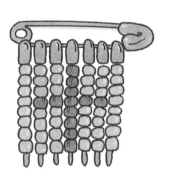

We know that God loves the world, because God gave us Jesus.

Thank you, God, for Jesus.

Hear or read
the Bible everyday.

Bible Favorites
Bookmark

white construction
paper

nickel
to trace
around

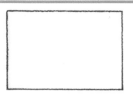

spool of thin
ribbon

white glue

scissors

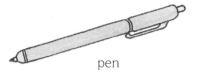

pen

what you do:

1 Cut three 2-foot (60-cm) lengths of ribbon.

2 Hold them together and fold them in half. Knot them together about 2 inches (5 cm) down from the fold.

3 Fold the construction paper in half. Use the nickel as a pattern to draw six circles on the white construction paper. Cut each stack of two circles out. Glue each stack of two circles together with the end of one of the ribbons between them. Let the glue dry.

4 Write the book and the chapter and verse numbers of one of your favorite Bible verses on each circle.

Place the marker in your Bible with each ribbon marking one of your favorite verses so you can find it easily.

Bible verse to read— Isaiah 34:16

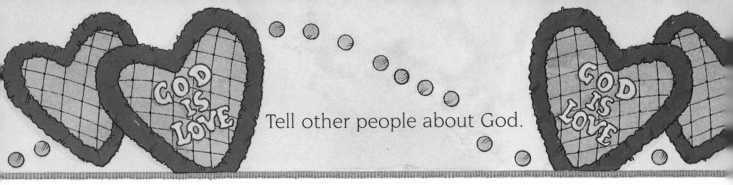

Tell other people about God.

Proclaim God's Word Necklace

you need:

red pipe cleaner

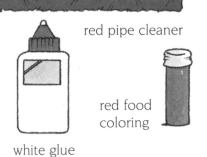

red food coloring

white glue

plastic margarine tub lid

paper cup and craft stick for mixing

yarn

macaroni letters

what you do:

1 Shape the end of the red pipe cleaner into a small heart. Trim off any extra pipe cleaner.

2 Cut a 2-foot (60-cm) length of yarn. Tie the yarn around the top of the heart, then tie the ends of the yarn together to make a necklace.

3 Rub some glue around the back of the pipe-cleaner heart and glue it to the plastic lid.

4 Pour a small amount of glue into the paper cup. Add a drop of red food coloring. Do not add more or the glue will become watery. The glue will dry a much darker shade of red than when it is wet. Mix the color into the glue.

5 Fill the heart with the colored glue. Let dry completely on a flat surface without being disturbed. This could take several days.

6 Find the macaroni letters to spell "God Is Love." Use white glue to glue them to the front of the heart. The glue will be clear when it dries.

Wear your necklace as a reminder to tell others about God.

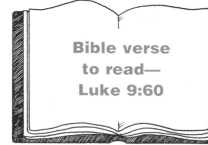

Bible verse to read— Luke 9:60

The Bible tells us that even a little faith in God can work great miracles.

Mustard Seed Necklace

you need:

 large-size wiggle eye

construction paper scrap

 mustard seed

thin gold cord

white glue

scissors

what you do:

1 Ask an adult to remove the back of a plastic wiggle eye so that you can use the clear plastic front.

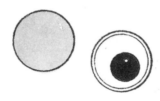

2 Trace around the eye on the construction paper and cut the tiny circle out.

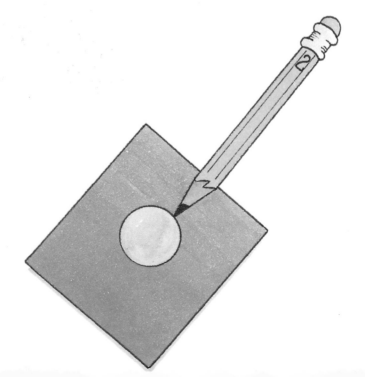

3 Put glue all the way around the edge of the paper circle. Carefully set the mustard seed in the center of the circle. Glue on the clear plastic from the wiggle eye over the circle. Let the glue dry.

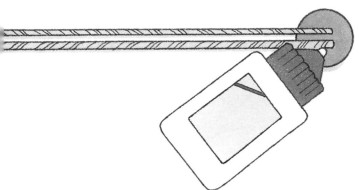

4 Cut a 2-foot (60-cm) length of gold cord. Glue the two ends of the cord to the back of the necklace to make a hanger.

When you wear the necklace, remember what the Bible tells us about faith as small as a mustard seed.

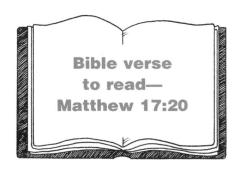

Bible verse to read— Matthew 17:20

God loves you!

Heart Frame Mask

you need:

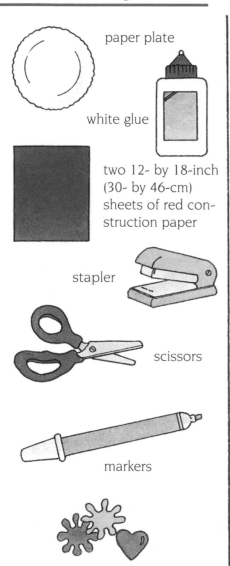

paper plate

white glue

two 12- by 18-inch (30- by 46-cm) sheets of red construction paper

stapler

scissors

markers

stickers

what you do:

1 Cut out the center part of the paper plate. This will be the base for the mask.

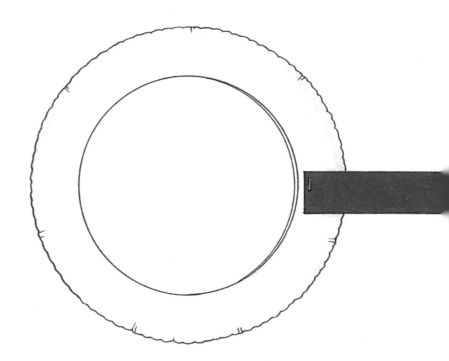

2 Cut a long 1 1/2-inch (3.75-cm)-wide strip from one sheet of the red paper. Staple one end of the strip to the top portion of the edge of the eating side of the paper-plate rim.

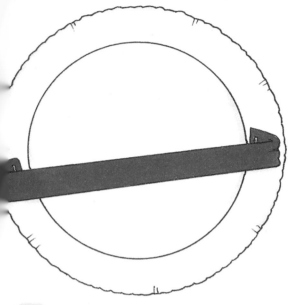

3 Hold the rim up to your face and wrap the rim around your head to make a band to hold the mask in place. Staple the strip to the other side of the rim and trim off any excess paper.

4 Fold the second sheet of paper in half to get a piece that is 9 by 12 inches (23 by 30 cm). Cut half a heart on the fold of the paper, making it as large as the paper will allow. Open up the paper to get a complete heart shape.

5 Place the plate rim on one side of the heart. The plate should not show from the front of the heart. If a tiny part of the plate shows at the top of the heart, just snip off that piece of plate. Trace around the hole in the plate on the heart. Cut the hole out of the heart.

6 Write on the top of the heart, "God Loves . . . " Decorate your heart any way you like, using stickers and/or markers.

7 Glue the heart to the front of the plate rim.

Wear your mask to show everyone that you know that God loves you.

Thank you, God, for loving me.

God tells us to share His love with others.

Love Notes

you need:

 clamp clothespin

 green marker

 macaroni craft letters

 white glue

 scissors

 red rickrack trim

 sticky-back magnet strip

what you do:

1 Color one side of the clothespin with the marker.

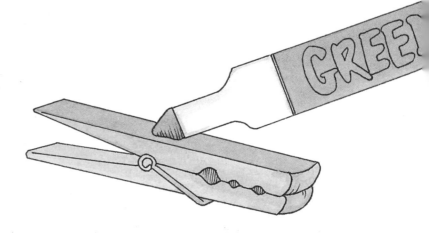

2 Cut a strip of rickrack as long as one side of the clothespin. Glue the rickrack over the colored side of the clothespin.

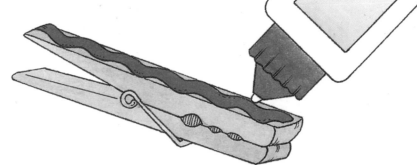

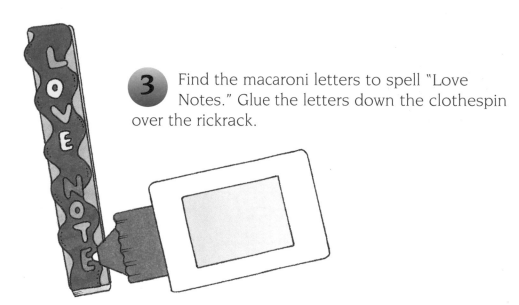

3 Find the macaroni letters to spell "Love Notes." Glue the letters down the clothespin over the rickrack.

4 Put a piece of sticky-back magnet on the back of the clothespin.

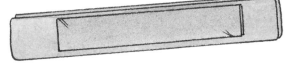

Stick the clothespin on your refrigerator. Use it to leave loving messages to the people in your family.

I love you! ☺

One way to show our love
and gratitude for Jesus is by
caring about others.

Prayer Necklace

you need:

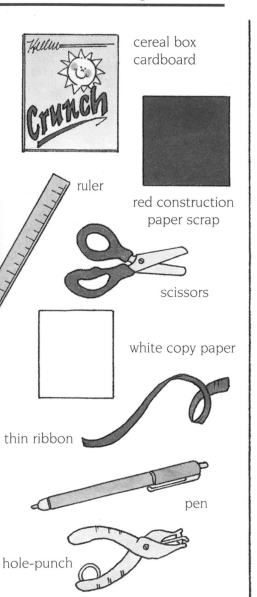

cereal box
cardboard

red construction
paper scrap

ruler

scissors

white copy paper

thin ribbon

pen

hole-punch

what you do:

1 Draw a 3-inch (8-cm)-high heart on the cardboard. Cut the heart out to use as a pattern.

2 Trace the heart on the red paper. Cut the heart out.

3 Trace the heart on the white paper. Cut out eight white hearts. You can stack the paper and cut out four hearts at a time.

4. Stack all the hearts together with the red heart on the bottom.

5. Fold the stack of hearts in half to make a heart book with the red heart forming the front and back cover.

6. Punch a hole in the top center of the folded hearts. Cut a 2-foot (60-cm) length of thin ribbon. Thread one end of the ribbon through the hole and tie the two ends together to make a necklace.

7. Use the pen to write "People I am praying for" on the front of the heart book.

People I am praying for

Tammy—hurt foot

Whenever you hear of someone in need of prayer, write the name down in your little prayer book as a reminder to pray for them.

A bedtime prayer is a wonderful ending to your day.

Glow-in-the-Dark Prayer Reminder

what you need:

cereal box cardboard

shredded Easter grass or green yarn bits

clear plastic cup

wooden stir stick

craft stick

glow-in-the-dark paint and a paintbrush

ruler

masking tape

gold glitter

scissors

white glue

plastic grocery bag to work on

what you do:

1 Trace around the rim of the cup on the cardboard. Cut the circle out.

2 Have a grown-up use large scissors to cut a 3-inch (8-cm) piece from the stick for the base of the cross. Cut a 2-inch (5-cm) piece for the crossbar of the cross. Cut the two ends of the second stick at an angle and then glue it across the first to form the cross.

3 Secure the cross to the center of the cardboard circle using masking tape.

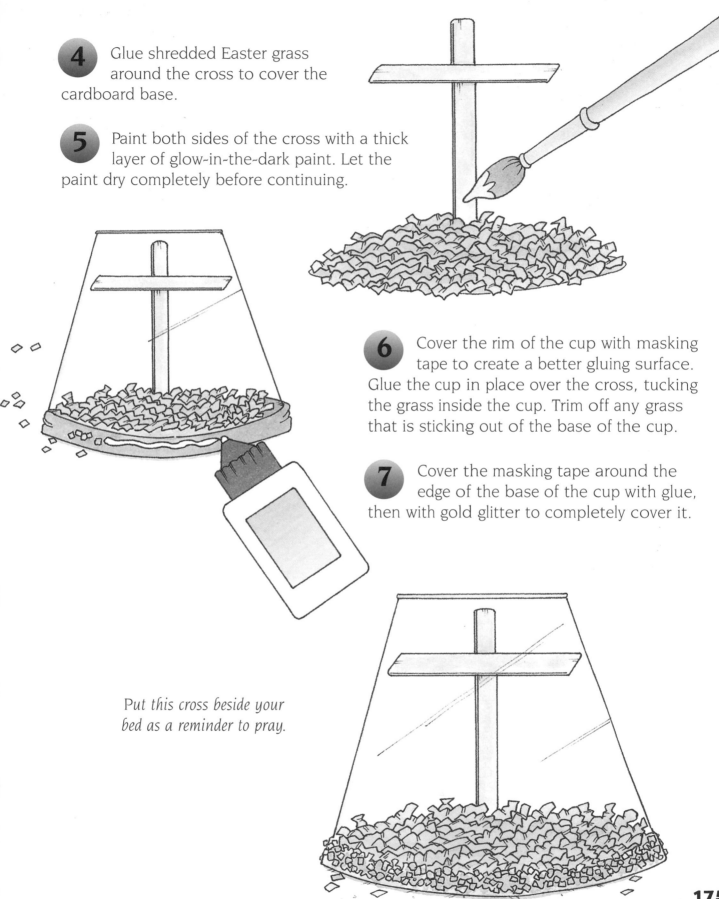

4 Glue shredded Easter grass around the cross to cover the cardboard base.

5 Paint both sides of the cross with a thick layer of glow-in-the-dark paint. Let the paint dry completely before continuing.

6 Cover the rim of the cup with masking tape to create a better gluing surface. Glue the cup in place over the cross, tucking the grass inside the cup. Trim off any grass that is sticking out of the base of the cup.

7 Cover the masking tape around the edge of the base of the cup with glue, then with gold glitter to completely cover it.

Put this cross beside your bed as a reminder to pray.

About the Author and Artist

More than thirty years as a Sunday School teacher and director of nursery school programs has given Kathy Ross extensive experience in guiding young children through crafts projects. Among the more than thirty-five craft books she has written are THE BEST BIRTHDAY PARTIES EVER, THE BEST HOLIDAY CRAFTS EVER, CRAFTS FOR ALL SEASONS, CRAFTS FROM YOUR FAVORITE FAIRY TALES, and CRAFTS FROM YOUR FAVORITE CHILDREN'S SONGS.

Sharon Lane Holm, a resident of Fairfield, Connecticut, won awards for her work in advertising design before shifting her concentration to children's books. Her recent books include SIDEWALK GAMES AROUND THE WORLD, HAPPY BIRTHDAY, EVERYWHERE!, and HAPPY NEW YEAR, EVERYWHERE! all by Arlene Erlbach, and BEAUTIFUL BATS by Linda Glaser.

Together, Kathy Ross and Sharon Lane Holm have also created the popular Holiday Crafts for Kids series as well as the Crafts for Kids Who Are Wild About series.